Top 100 Pasta Dishes

Annabel Karmel

Top 100 Pasta Dishes

Easy everyday recipes that children will love

ATRIA PAPERBACK

New York   London   Toronto   Sydney   New Delhi

To my children, Nicholas, Lara, and Scarlett

An Imprint of Simon & Schuster, Inc.
1230 Avenue of the Americas
New York, NY 10020

First Atria Paperback edition April 2020

ATRIA PAPERBACK and colophon are trademarks of Simon & Schuster, Inc.

For information about special discounts for bulk purchases,
please contact Simon & Schuster Special Sales at
1-866-506-1949 or business@simonandschuster.com.

The Simon & Schuster Speakers Bureau can bring authors
to your live event. For more information or to book an event,
contact the Simon & Schuster Speakers Bureau at
1-866-248-3049 or visit our website at www.simonspeakers.com.

Manufactured in the United States of America

1   3   5   7   9   10   8   6   4   2

The Library of Congress has cataloged the hardcover edition as follows:
Karmel, Annabel.
Top 100 pasta dishes : easy everyday recipes that children will love / Annabel Karmel.
      p.   cm.
1. Cooking (Pasta)   2. Quick and easy cooking.   3. Cookbooks.
   I. Title.   II. Title: Top one hundred pasta dishes.
         TX809.M17K37   2011
641.8'22—dc22   2011014410

ISBN 978-1-4516-0791-8
ISBN 978-1-9821-4883-6 (pbk)
ISBN 978-1-4516-0809-0 (ebook)

Contents

Pasta shells with salmon and broccoli

Fish is good for the brain; omega-3 essential fatty acids are found in oily fish and make up 40 percent of the brain. A baby's brain grows rapidly between birth and three years, and most of this growth takes place in the first year, so it's important to introduce fish such as salmon early on. Fish is quick and easy to prepare and delicious combined with root vegetables. (Note: For babies younger than a year, using *unsalted* broth is recommended.)

2 ounces salmon fillet, skinned
⅔ cup vegetable or chicken broth
¼ cup small pasta shells
a pat of butter
½ small onion, finely chopped
2 teaspoons all-purpose flour
½ cup milk
½ cup roughly chopped broccoli
3 tablespoons crème fraîche or heavy cream
3 tablespoons grated Parmesan cheese
1 teaspoon lemon juice
½ teaspoon chopped fresh dill
½ teaspoon chopped fresh chives

★ To cook the salmon, either poach the fish in a little of the broth over low heat for 3 to 4 minutes, until it flakes easily with a fork, or cook in a microwave with a couple of tablespoons of the broth for about 2 minutes.

★ Meanwhile, cook the pasta following the instructions on the package. Drain.

★ To make the sauce, melt the butter in a saucepan. Add the onion and sauté for 3 to 4 minutes, just until soft. Add the flour and mix together, then blend in the remaining broth and the milk. Bring to a boil. Add the broccoli and simmer, covered, for 5 to 6 minutes until soft.

★ Whiz in a food processor until smooth. Return to the pan and stir in the crème fraîche, Parmesan, lemon juice, herbs, and cooked salmon. Simmer for 2 minutes. Serve the drained pasta with the sauce.

Pasta stars with carrot and tomato

Stir these tiny pasta stars into your baby's favorite puree for a gradual introduction to more lumpy food. Interestingly, carrots are more nutritious when cooked with a little butter or oil, as the beta-carotene they contain is absorbed more readily. The same is true of tomatoes; they are rich in lycopene, a powerful antioxidant that is better absorbed by our bodies when tomatoes are cooked with a little oil or butter.

2 medium carrots, sliced (1 cup)
1 tablespoon butter
3 medium tomatoes, peeled, seeded, and quartered
scant ½ cup grated Cheddar cheese
2 fresh basil leaves, torn into pieces
¼ cup small pasta stars

★ Steam the carrots for about 20 minutes, or until tender. Heat the butter in a separate pan, then add the tomatoes and sauté until mushy. Remove from the heat and stir in the cheese until melted; add the fresh basil.

★ Meanwhile, cook the pasta stars following the instructions on the package. Drain.

★ Puree the cooked carrots together with 3 tablespoons of the liquid from the bottom of the steamer using a handheld blender. Blend together with the tomato and cheese mixture and stir in the drained pasta stars.

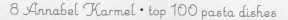

☺ SUITABLE FROM 7 MONTHS

◡ MAKES 6 PORTIONS

🕓 PREPARATION TIME: 10 MINUTES / COOKING TIME: 30 MINUTES

❄ SAUCE SUITABLE FOR FREEZING

Tomato, sweet potato, and cheese sauce with pasta shells

This delicious tomato sauce is enriched with vegetables. It is very versatile; you can mix it with pasta, as here, or blend it together with cooked fish or chicken.

1 tablespoon olive oil
1 medium onion, chopped
1 garlic clove, chopped
1 medium sweet potato, peeled and chopped (1²⁄₃ cups)
2 medium carrots, sliced (1 cup)
one 14-ounce can diced tomatoes
³⁄₄ cup vegetable broth or water
²⁄₃ cup small pasta shells
²⁄₃ cup grated Cheddar cheese

★ Heat the oil in a saucepan and sauté the onion for about 4 minutes, or until softened. Add the garlic and sauté for 1 minute more. Stir in the sweet potato and carrots, then stir in the tomatoes and vegetable broth or water. Bring to a boil, stirring, cover the pan, and simmer for about 30 minutes, or until the vegetables are tender.
★ Meanwhile, cook the pasta following the instructions on the package. Drain.
★ Once cooked, let the sauce cool slightly, then blend the sauce to a puree and stir in the cheese until melted. Mix the drained pasta with the sauce.

SUITABLE FROM 7 MONTHS

MAKES 4 PORTIONS

PREPARATION TIME: 5 MINUTES / COOKING TIME: 20 MINUTES

SUITABLE FOR FREEZING

Pasta with tomato and mascarpone sauce

Five different vegetables are blended into this tasty tomato sauce. Mascarpone is good for babies, as they need proportionately more fat in their diets than adults due to their rapid growth rate. If you don't have any, use heavy cream or cream cheese instead.

1 tablespoon olive oil
1 medium red onion, chopped
¼ cup diced carrot
¼ cup diced zucchini
2 tablespoons diced celery
1 garlic clove, crushed
½ cup chopped button mushrooms
one 14-ounce can crushed or diced
   tomatoes
2 tablespoons apple juice
⅓ cup small pasta shells
2 tablespoons torn fresh basil
   (optional)
3 tablespoons mascarpone cheese
3 tablespoons grated Parmesan
   cheese

★ Heat the oil in a saucepan and sauté the onion, carrot, zucchini, and celery for 5 minutes. Add the garlic and sauté for 1 minute. Add the button mushrooms and sauté for 2 minutes. Stir in the crushed or diced tomatoes with the apple juice and simmer for 10 minutes with the lid on, stirring occasionally.

★ Meanwhile, cook the pasta shells following the instructions on the package. Drain.

★ Remove the tomato sauce from the heat, add the basil (if using), and blend in a food processor. Return to the pan and stir in the mascarpone and Parmesan. Stir the drained pasta into the sauce.

VARIATION: To make a creamy tomato-chicken bolognese sauce, simply add ½ cup diced cooked chicken breast at the same time as the mushrooms.

SUITABLE FROM 8 MONTHS

MAKES 4 PORTIONS

PREPARATION TIME: 8 MINUTES /
COOKING TIME: 15 MINUTES

SUITABLE FOR FREEZING

SUITABLE FROM 9 MONTHS

MAKES 4 PORTIONS

PREPARATION TIME: 8 MINUTES /
COOKING TIME: 18 MINUTES

SUITABLE FOR FREEZING

Mushroom and spinach pasta

⅓ cup small pasta shells
1 tablespoon butter
¼ cup finely diced onion
½ cup finely diced cremini
　　mushrooms
1 garlic clove, crushed
1 tablespoon all-purpose flour
1 cup milk
¼ teaspoon chopped fresh thyme
⅓ cup grated Parmesan cheese
½ cup finely chopped baby spinach

★ Cook the pasta following the instructions on the package. Drain.
★ Melt the butter in a saucepan, add the onion, cover, and sauté
for 8 minutes, or until softened. Add the mushrooms and cook for
3 minutes. Add the garlic and cook for 2 minutes. Add the flour, then
add the milk, stirring until thickened. Add the thyme, Parmesan,
and spinach and stir until wilted.
★ Stir in the drained pasta.

Chicken and corn pasta

⅓ cup small pasta shells
1 tablespoon butter
¼ cup finely diced onion
4 ounces boneless, skinless chicken
　　breast, cut into small pieces
4 teaspoons all-purpose flour
1 cup milk
3 tablespoons drained canned or
　　frozen corn kernels
½ teaspoon Dijon mustard
¼ cup grated Parmesan cheese
1 teaspoon finely chopped fresh chives

★ Cook the pasta following the instructions on the package. Drain.
★ To make the sauce, melt the butter in a saucepan, then add
the onion, cover, and cook gently for about 8 minutes, or until soft.
Add the chicken and sauté for 2 minutes. Add the flour, stir over the
heat for 1 minute, then add the milk, stirring until thickened. Add
the corn and mustard and simmer for 5 minutes, then remove from
the heat and add the Parmesan and chives.
★ Stir in the drained pasta.

Hidden vegetable bolognese

This bolognese is good with pasta shapes, or you could mix it with some potatoes mashed with a little butter and milk and maybe just a little grated Cheddar. You could also make this with ground turkey or chicken.

1 tablespoon olive oil
2 shallots, chopped (about ⅓ cup)
⅓ cup diced carrot
2 tablespoons diced celery
1 small garlic clove, crushed
½ cup chopped peeled butternut squash
half a 14-ounce can diced tomatoes
6 ounces lean ground beef
1 teaspoon tomato paste
½ cup beef or chicken broth, or water, plus extra as needed
1 teaspoon fresh thyme leaves
⅓ cup pasta stars

★ Heat the oil in a saucepan and sauté the shallots, carrot, and celery over low heat for 7 to 8 minutes, until softened. Add the garlic and cook for 30 seconds. Add the butternut squash, pour in the diced tomatoes, and cook for 5 minutes.

★ Meanwhile, brown the ground beef in a skillet with no oil. Transfer the vegetables to a food processor and blend until smooth. Put the blended vegetables back in the pan; add the tomato paste, broth, thyme, and the browned meat. Cover and cook for 12 to 15 minutes, adding a little more broth if necessary.

★ Meanwhile, cook the pasta stars following the instructions on the package. Once cooked, drain and toss with the sauce.

☻ SUITABLE FROM 7 MONTHS

🥣 MAKES 4 PORTIONS

🕐 PREPARATION TIME: 8 MINUTES / COOKING TIME: 37 MINUTES

❄ SUITABLE FOR FREEZING

Tomato sauce with butternut squash and red lentils

This tasty sauce is enriched with lentils and butternut squash. Lentils are a good cheap source of protein and iron and as such are important in a vegetarian diet. Butternut squash is rich in beta-carotene, which is important for growth, healthy skin, and good vision. With nonmeat sources of iron such as lentils, whole-grain cereals, and green leafy vegetables, you need to give vitamin C at the same meal to help the absorption of iron.

1 tablespoon olive oil
⅓ cup chopped onion
½ cup chopped carrot
2 tablespoons chopped celery
¼ cup split red lentils
scant 1 cup chopped peeled
    butternut squash
half a 14-ounce can crushed or
    diced tomatoes
⅔ cup water
⅓ cup small pasta shells
scant ½ cup grated sharp Cheddar
    cheese

★ Heat the oil in a saucepan and sauté the onion, carrot, and celery for 5 minutes.

★ Rinse and drain the lentils and add to the pan. Add the butternut squash and cook, stirring, for 1 minute. Pour in the crushed or diced tomatoes and the water. Cover and cook over low heat for about 30 minutes.

★ Meanwhile, cook the pasta following the instructions on the package. Drain.

★ Remove the squash and lentils mixture from the heat and stir in the cheese until melted. Puree in a blender, then return to the pan and stir in the drained pasta.

☺ SUITABLE FROM 8 MONTHS

🥣 MAKES 4 PORTIONS

🕐 PREPARATION TIME: 10 MINUTES /
COOKING TIME: 18 MINUTES

❄ SUITABLE FOR FREEZING

☺ SUITABLE FROM 7 MONTHS

🥣 MAKES 2 PORTIONS

🕐 PREPARATION TIME: 5 MINUTES /
COOKING TIME: 9 MINUTES

❄ NOT SUITABLE FOR FREEZING

Baby vegetable pasta

As your baby gets older, it is important to encourage him to chew, so dice vegetables instead of pureeing them. Frozen peas and corn kernels are good standbys to keep in your freezer.

⅓ cup small pasta shells
1 tablespoon butter
¼ cup finely chopped onion
3 tablespoons finely diced carrot
2 tablespoons finely diced red bell pepper
¼ cup frozen corn kernels
¼ cup frozen peas
1 tablespoon all-purpose flour
1 cup vegetable broth
2 tablespoons chopped fresh basil
1 teaspoon lemon juice
⅓ cup grated Parmesan cheese

★ Cook the pasta following the instructions on the package. Drain.
★ Melt the butter in a saucepan. Add the onion, carrot, and bell pepper, cover, and cook gently for 10 minutes, or until nearly soft. Add the corn and peas and sauté for 2 minutes. Add the flour, then add the broth, stirring until thickened. Simmer for 3 minutes, then add the basil, lemon juice, and Parmesan.
★ Stir in the drained pasta.

Confetti pasta

¼ cup orzo or other small pasta shapes
3 tablespoons diced carrot
¼ cup frozen peas
1½ tablespoons heavy cream
3 tablespoons grated Parmesan cheese

★ Cook the pasta following the instructions on the package. Add the diced carrot for the last 6 minutes; add the peas for the last 2 to 3 minutes, then drain.
★ Stir the cream and Parmesan into the pasta and serve.

Cheese sauce with butternut squash

If you have time, it's nice to infuse the milk to give it extra flavor, but you can skip this step if you prefer. For older babies, I blend only half the vegetables with the sauce and leave the remainder chunky so the sauce has some texture.

1⅔ cups milk
½ medium onion, cut into wedges
1 bay leaf
3 fresh parsley sprigs
3 black peppercorns
1 tablespoon butter
1 cup diced peeled butternut squash
1 tablespoon all-purpose flour
⅓ cup small pasta shells
¾ teaspoon Dijon mustard
3 tablespoons grated Parmesan cheese
3 tablespoons grated sharp Cheddar cheese

★ First, infuse the milk: Put the milk, onion wedges, bay leaf, parsley sprigs, and peppercorns into a saucepan. Bring to a boil and simmer gently for 20 to 30 minutes, then strain into a pitcher.

★ Melt the butter in a clean saucepan. Add the squash and sauté for 5 minutes. Add the flour, then the strained milk, stirring until thickened. Simmer for 10 minutes, or until the ingredients are soft.

★ Meanwhile, cook the pasta following the instructions on the package. Drain.

★ Whiz the vegetables and sauce in a food processor until smooth. For older babies, whiz the sauce with half the vegetables and leave the other half diced. Add the mustard and cheeses. Stir in the drained pasta.

☺ SUITABLE FROM 7 MONTHS

♨ MAKES 3 PORTIONS

🕐 PREPARATION TIME: 10 MINUTES /
   COOKING TIME: 25 MINUTES

❄ SUITABLE FOR FREEZING

☺ SUITABLE FROM 9 MONTHS

♨ MAKES 4 PORTIONS

🕐 PREPARATION TIME: 8 MINUTES/
   COOKING TIME: 15 MINUTES

❄ SUITABLE FOR FREEZING

Little stars with ground beef

⅓ cup pasta stars
1 tablespoon butter
3 tablespoons finely diced onion
⅓ cup finely diced carrot
2 tablespoons finely diced celery
4 ounces lean ground beef
½ teaspoon red currant jelly
   (optional)
1 tablespoon all-purpose flour
1 cup beef broth
1 teaspoon tomato paste
1 teaspoon Worcestershire sauce
½ teaspoon fresh thyme leaves

★ Cook the pasta following the instructions on the package. Drain.
★ Melt the butter in a saucepan and add the onion, carrot, and celery and sauté for 5 minutes. Add the ground beef to the vegetables and brown for 5 minutes, breaking up the lumps with a fork as you stir. Add the red currant jelly, if using, and sauté for 1 minute. Add the flour, then the broth, tomato paste, Worcestershire sauce, and thyme. Simmer for 10 minutes, uncovered.
★ Stir in the drained pasta.

Cauliflower, broccoli, and pea pasta

⅓ cup small pasta shells
1 tablespoon butter
¼ cup finely chopped onion
½ cup small cauliflower florets
½ cup small broccoli florets
⅓ cup frozen peas
1 tablespoon all-purpose flour
1 cup milk
⅓ cup grated Parmesan cheese
½ teaspoon Dijon mustard

★ Cook the pasta following the instructions on the package. Drain.
★ Melt the butter in a saucepan, add the onion, and sauté for 5 minutes. Add the cauliflower, broccoli, and peas. Sauté for 5 minutes, then add the flour and milk, stirring until thickened. Simmer for a few minutes, then spoon half of the mixture into a bowl.
★ Whiz the remaining mixture in the pan using a handheld blender until smooth. Stir in the Parmesan and mustard, then return the reserved unblended mixture to the pan with the drained pasta.

- SUITABLE FROM 9 MONTHS
- MAKES 4 PORTIONS
- PREPARATION TIME: 8 MINUTES / COOKING TIME: 20 MINUTES
- SUITABLE FOR FREEZING

Fruity chicken curry with pasta

Korma curry paste has a slightly sweet flavor that is ideal for younger palates. Dried apricots are rich in beta-carotene and also contain iron. I prefer to use organic dried apricots, which are brown in color; commercial ones are often treated with sulfur dioxide (to preserve their bright orange color), which can trigger an asthma attack in susceptible babies.

⅓ cup small pasta shells
2 teaspoons canola oil
¼ cup finely diced onion
¼ teaspoon grated peeled fresh ginger
2 teaspoons mild korma curry paste (such as Patak's)
⅔ cup chicken broth
½ cup coconut milk
4 roughly chopped dried apricots
⅓ cup finely diced peeled butternut squash
4 ounces boneless, skinless chicken breast, cut into small pieces

★ Cook the pasta following the instructions on the package. Drain.

★ Heat 1 teaspoon of the oil in a saucepan. Add the onion and ginger and sauté for 5 minutes. Add the curry paste, then the broth and coconut milk. Add the apricots and squash. Bring to a boil, then simmer, covered, for 10 minutes, or until the squash is tender. Whiz until smooth using a handheld blender.

★ Heat the remaining 1 teaspoon oil in a wok or skillet and sauté the chicken for 3 to 4 minutes, or until cooked through. Add the sauce, then stir in the drained pasta.

SUITABLE FROM 8 MONTHS

MAKES 3 PORTIONS

PREPARATION TIME: 8 MINUTES / COOKING TIME: 25 MINUTES

SUITABLE FOR FREEZING

Tomato and Mediterranean vegetable sauce

Adding diced apple and apple juice gives a sweetness to this sauce that appeals to babies. If you don't have any eggplant, use diced carrot or butternut squash instead, but you will need to add this together with the onion so that it cooks long enough to soften.

⅓ cup small pasta shells
2 teaspoons olive oil
⅓ cup finely chopped onion
1 small garlic clove, crushed
2 tablespoons finely diced red bell pepper
2 tablespoons finely diced eggplant
2 tablespoons finely diced celery
⅓ cup finely diced zucchini
2 tablespoons finely diced peeled apple
½ cup apple juice (I use a natural, unfiltered apple juice)
1¼ cups canned diced tomatoes
1 teaspoon ketchup
1 tablespoon chopped fresh basil

★ Cook the pasta following the instructions on the package. Drain.
★ Heat the oil in a saucepan, add the onion, and sauté for 5 minutes. Add the garlic and cook for 1 minute; then add the bell pepper, eggplant, celery, zucchini, and apple and sauté for 5 minutes. Next, add the apple juice, tomatoes, and ketchup. Bring to a boil, then simmer, covered, for 10 minutes.
★ Add the basil and stir in the drained pasta.

Fillet of fish with carrot, tomato, and cheese sauce

1¼ cups chopped carrot
¼ cup small pasta shells
4 ounces skinless flounder, gray sole, or cod fillet
1 tablespoon milk, plus extra as needed
2 tablespoons butter, plus extra as needed
3 medium tomatoes, peeled, seeded, and chopped
scant ½ cup grated Cheddar cheese

★ Steam the carrot for about 10 minutes, or until tender.
★ Cook the pasta following the package instructions. Drain.
★ Meanwhile, place the fish in a microwave-safe dish, add the milk, dot with butter, and cover, leaving an air vent. Microwave on high for about 1½ minutes. Alternatively, poach the fish in a saucepan of milk for a couple of minutes.
★ Melt the 2 tablespoons butter in a saucepan and cook the tomatoes for 3 minutes, then stir in the cheese until melted. Blend the fish together with the steamed carrot and the tomato and cheese sauce. Stir in the drained pasta.

Creamy spinach sauce

¼ cup small pasta shells
8 ounces fresh spinach or 5 ounces frozen whole leaf spinach (half a 10-ounce box)
a pat of butter
2 tablespoons milk
2 tablespoons cream cheese
¼ cup grated Parmesan cheese

★ Cook the pasta following the package instructions. Drain.
★ Carefully wash the fresh spinach and cook with the water just clinging to its leaves in a saucepan over low heat, stirring occasionally, until wilted. Gently press out the excess water. If using frozen spinach, cook following the package instructions.
★ Melt the butter in a small saucepan and sauté the spinach, then stir in the milk and cheeses. Transfer the mixture to a food processor and chop finely. Mix with the drained pasta.

TODDLER

Chicken soup with alphabet pasta

According to food historians, chicken soup was already being prescribed as a cure for the common cold in ancient Egypt in the tenth century BCE. Also known as Jewish penicillin, it is thought to be a natural remedy for colds and flu. Chicken soup is good for a sick child, as it is easy to digest and will help to keep up fluid levels.

1 tablespoon butter
2 shallots, finely chopped
1 medium carrot, diced
4 cups chicken broth
1 teaspoon soy sauce
6 ounces skinless, boneless chicken breast, cut into small cubes
1 cup canned corn kernels, drained
¼ cup alphabet pasta (or similar shapes, such as stars)
¾ cup frozen peas
salt and freshly ground black pepper
chopped fresh parsley, to serve (optional)

★ Melt the butter in a large saucepan and sauté the shallots and carrot for 8 to 10 minutes, until the shallots have softened. Add the broth and soy sauce, bring to a boil, and boil for 5 minutes, or until the carrot is soft. Turn the heat down to very low, add the chicken and corn, and cook very gently for 5 minutes, or until the chicken has cooked through. Try not to let the soup boil at all, as boiling can make the chicken a little tough.

★ Meanwhile, cook the pasta following the instructions on the package. Drain.

★ Add the drained pasta plus the peas to the soup. Cook for 2 to 3 minutes more, until the peas have just thawed. Season well with a little salt and pepper. Ladle into warm bowls.

★ You can serve the soup garnished with a little chopped parsley if you like.

Spaghetti with a mild curried-chicken sauce

A mild fruity curry is popular with children. This one is very simple to make and can be served with pasta or rice.

8 ounces spaghetti
2 tablespoons canola oil
1 large onion, sliced
1 garlic clove, crushed
1½ tablespoons mild korma curry
   paste (such as Patak's)
1½ teaspoons mango chutney
1 tablespoon tomato paste
8 ounces skinless, boneless chicken
   breast, cut into small strips
1 tablespoon chopped fresh parsley
1¼ cups chicken broth
3 tomatoes, peeled, seeded,
   and roughly chopped
¾ cup frozen peas
3 tablespoons heavy cream
salt and freshly ground
   black pepper

★ Cook the spaghetti following the instructions on the package. Drain.

★ Heat the oil in a large saucepan and sauté the onion and garlic for 3 to 4 minutes, until the onion has softened. Add the korma paste, mango chutney, and tomato paste and cook for 1 minute, stirring occasionally. Add the chicken and parsley and cook, stirring, for 2 minutes; then add the broth, chopped tomatoes, and peas and cook for 3 minutes. Stir in the cream and season with a little salt and pepper.

★ Toss the drained pasta with the sauce.

Chicken and butternut squash pasta risotto

Orzo is pasta that looks like grains of rice; however, you could make this using other small pasta shapes. Roasting the squash in the oven gives it a naturally sweet taste. If you prefer, you could leave out the mushrooms and add some frozen peas toward the end instead.

¼ medium butternut squash, peeled, seeded, and cut into small cubes (about 12 ounces)
2 tablespoons olive oil
salt and freshly ground black pepper
1⅓ cups sliced button mushrooms
1⅓ cups orzo or other small pasta shapes
5 cups chicken broth
2 tablespoons butter
1 large onion, finely chopped
1 leek, trimmed, rinsed, and finely chopped
1 garlic clove, crushed
2 teaspoons chopped fresh thyme leaves
1 cup diced cooked chicken breast
¼ cup grated Parmesan cheese
⅓ cup crème fraîche or heavy cream

★ Preheat the oven to 400°F.

★ Toss the squash in 1 tablespoon of the olive oil and season with salt and pepper. Place on a baking sheet and roast in the oven for 20 to 25 minutes, until cooked and lightly golden brown.

★ Heat the remaining 1 tablespoon oil in a large saucepan and sauté the mushrooms for 5 to 6 minutes, until golden brown. Remove from the pan and set aside.

★ Meanwhile, cook the orzo or pasta in the broth following the instructions on the package. Drain, reserving 2 tablespoons of the broth.

★ Melt the butter in the saucepan, add the onion, leek, and garlic, and sauté for 5 minutes. Add the thyme and chicken and then the Parmesan, reserved broth, and crème fraîche or cream. Simmer for 1 minute, then add the pasta, butternut squash, and the mushrooms and toss together. Season well with black pepper.

☺ SUITABLE FROM 18 MONTHS

◡ MAKES 4 PORTIONS

🕐 PREPARATION TIME: 20 MINUTES / COOKING TIME: 15 MINUTES

❋ MEATBALLS AND SAUCE SUITABLE FOR FREEZING

Turkey meatballs with spaghetti

When my son, Nicholas, was a toddler, I couldn't get him to eat chicken, but as he liked apple, I made mini chicken balls with grated apple—and he loved them. These meatballs also make good finger food served without the sauce and with the spaghetti on the side.

MEATBALLS
1 tablespoon olive oil
1 medium onion, finely chopped
8 ounces ground turkey or chicken
¾ cup fresh bread crumbs
1 apple, peeled and grated
4 fresh sage leaves
1 teaspoon fresh thyme leaves or
   ¼ teaspoon dried thyme
salt and freshly ground black pepper
all-purpose flour, for dusting

8 ounces spaghetti

SAUCE
2 tablespoons olive oil
1 small red onion, chopped
1 garlic clove, crushed
¼ teaspoon dried oregano
1 tomato, seeded and chopped
one 14-ounce can diced tomatoes
pinch of sugar

★ Preheat the oven to 350°F.

★ To make the turkey meatballs, heat the oil in a skillet and sauté the onion for about 4 minutes. Let cool, then mix together the sautéed onion, ground turkey or chicken, bread crumbs, grated apple, sage, and thyme and season to taste with salt and pepper. Put the mixture into a food processor and pulse for a couple of seconds. Using floured hands, form into about 12 meatballs. Arrange them on a baking sheet and bake for 10 minutes.

★ Meanwhile, cook the spaghetti following the instructions on the package. Drain.

★ To make the sauce, heat the oil in a saucepan and sauté the red onion for about 4 minutes; add the garlic and cook for 30 seconds. Add the oregano and tomato and sauté for 3 to 4 minutes, until the tomato turns mushy. Add the canned tomatoes and cook for 5 minutes. Add a pinch of sugar and season to taste. Stir in the meatballs.

★ Toss with the drained spaghetti and carefully mix.

VARIATION: Try making these with the same quantity of ground beef or chicken instead of turkey.

☺ SUITABLE FROM 18 MONTHS

🥣 MAKES 4 PORTIONS

🕐 PREPARATION TIME: 8 MINUTES / COOKING TIME: 24 MINUTES

❄ SUITABLE FOR FREEZING

Chicken bolognese

Traditional bolognese is made with ground beef, but a bolognese made with ground chicken (preferably using thigh meat) is also delicious, and this is a popular dish with my children. Fresh thyme adds a nice flavor to the chicken. If you don't have tomato paste, you can use ketchup.

8 ounces penne or fusilli pasta
1 tablespoon olive oil
1 small onion, finely chopped
1 small carrot, grated
1 apple, peeled and grated
8 ounces ground chicken
   (I use chicken thigh meat)
1 garlic clove, crushed
1¼ cups tomato sauce
¾ cup chicken broth
1 teaspoon tomato paste
1 teaspoon fresh thyme leaves or
   ¼ teaspoon dried thyme
salt and freshly ground
   black pepper

★ Cook the pasta following the instructions on the package. Drain.
★ Heat the oil in a saucepan. Add the onion and sauté for 5 minutes. Add the carrot and apple and sauté for another 5 minutes. Add the chicken and garlic and lightly sauté while breaking up the meat. Add the tomato sauce, broth, tomato paste, and thyme. Bring to a boil, then simmer, covered, for 10 minutes.
★ Season to taste with salt and pepper and serve with the cooked pasta.

SUITABLE FROM 1 YEAR

MAKES 6 TO 8 PORTIONS

PREPARATION TIME: 12 MINUTES / COOKING TIME: 30 MINUTES

NOT SUITABLE FOR FREEZING

Four-cheese macaroni

This is a sort of cheat's way of making cheese sauce. If you can't find Taleggio, use fontina cheese instead.

2 cups elbow macaroni
½ cup mascarpone cheese
⅔ cup whole milk
4 ounces Taleggio cheese,
    rind removed and cheese cubed
½ cup grated Gruyère cheese
½ teaspoon Dijon mustard
large pinch of grated nutmeg
1 cup grated Parmesan cheese
salt and freshly ground black
    pepper
⅓ cup fresh bread crumbs

★ Cook the macaroni following the instructions on the package. Drain and rinse with cold water. Allow to drain in the colander while you make the sauce.

★ Preheat the oven to 400°F.

★ Put the mascarpone and the milk in a saucepan and heat gently until the mascarpone has melted. Add the Taleggio, Gruyère, mustard, and nutmeg and heat, stirring the cheese until melted (be patient, as it takes a few minutes).

★ Set aside a handful of the Parmesan and add the rest to the sauce. Stir until melted, then season with salt and black pepper and stir in the drained pasta; transfer to a baking dish.

★ Mix the reserved Parmesan and bread crumbs and season with salt and pepper. Sprinkle this over the macaroni and cheese and bake for 20 minutes, or until golden on top and bubbling. (Brown it for a few minutes under a preheated broiler if you wish.)

VARIATION: You can also add strips of ham or small broccoli florets that have been lightly blanched or steamed.

Oodles of noodles

Thin noodles with ribbons of colorful vegetables.

4 ounces medium Chinese egg noodles (chow mein noodles)
½ large carrot
½ medium zucchini, trimmed
½ small leek, white part only, rinsed
¼ each red, yellow, and orange bell peppers, seeded
1½ tablespoons canola oil
1 medium onion, thinly sliced
1 garlic clove, crushed
⅔ cup bean sprouts
1½ tablespoons teriyaki sauce
salt and freshly ground black pepper

★ Cook the noodles following the package instructions. Drain.
★ Prepare the carrot, zucchini, leek, and bell peppers by cutting them into thin strips like ribbons—you can cut the carrot and zucchini simply by using a vegetable peeler.
★ Heat the oil in a large skillet or a wok and stir-fry the onion, carrot, and leek for 5 minutes. Add the bell peppers, zucchini, and garlic and cook for 5 minutes. Add the bean sprouts and drained noodles. Pour in the teriyaki sauce. Season to taste with salt and pepper and serve.

VARIATION: This is also wonderful with marinated chicken. To make the marinade, mix together in a bowl 2 tablespoons soy sauce, 2 tablespoons mirin, 1 teaspoon sugar, and 1 teaspoon Asian sesame oil. Cut 2 skinless, boneless chicken breasts into thin strips and add to the marinade. Stir well, then allow to marinate for 20 minutes. Sauté the chicken for 4 to 5 minutes, or until cooked through. Add the cooked chicken at the point when you add the bean sprouts and drained noodles.

SUITABLE FROM 1 YEAR

MAKES 4 TO 6 PORTIONS

PREPARATION TIME: 15 MINUTES / COOKING TIME: 15 MINUTES

SUITABLE FOR FREEZING

Minestrone with pasta shells

You can make up your own combination of vegetables depending on what your child likes. If your child isn't keen on cannellini beans, leave them out, and if he doesn't like cabbage, substitute frozen peas.

¾ cup small pasta shells
2 tablespoons olive oil
½ large onion, chopped
½ large carrot, diced
2 celery stalks, diced
2 garlic cloves, chopped or crushed
½ leek, white part only, rinsed and diced
4 cups vegetable broth
2 ounces green beans, cut into ½-inch lengths
½ zucchini, diced
¾ cup finely shredded Savoy cabbage
⅓ cup cannellini beans, drained (canned are fine)
1 large tomato, seeded and diced
1½ tablespoons fresh pesto (see page 122) or good-quality store-bought
salt and freshly ground black pepper

★ Cook the pasta shells following the instructions on the package. Drain.

★ Heat the oil in a large saucepan and sauté the onion, carrot, and celery for 2 to 3 minutes, until soft. Add the garlic and cook for 30 seconds. Add the leek and sauté for 2 minutes.

★ Add the broth and simmer for 5 minutes. Add the green beans and cook for 1 minute. Add the zucchini, cabbage, drained pasta, cannellini beans, and tomato and simmer for 2 minutes. Stir in the pesto and season to taste with salt and pepper.

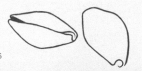

- SUITABLE FROM 1 YEAR
- MAKES 4 PORTIONS
- PREPARATION TIME: 12 MINUTES / COOKING TIME: 30 MINUTES
- SUITABLE FOR FREEZING

Butternut squash gratin with penne

Butternut squash is rich in beta-carotene, and it tastes delicious mixed with a cheese sauce and pasta, then baked in the oven with a golden bread crumb topping.

1 medium butternut squash
6 ounces penne pasta

SAUCE
2 tablespoons butter, plus extra for greasing
3 tablespoons all-purpose flour
1½ cups milk
½ cup grated Gruyère cheese
1 cup grated Parmesan cheese
¼ cup heavy cream
salt and freshly ground black pepper
grated nutmeg

1 cup fresh bread crumbs
salt and freshly ground black pepper

★ Cut the butternut squash in half, remove the seeds and fiber, peel, then chop into ¾-inch cubes. Steam for about 8 minutes (not too long, as it will be cooked again in the oven).

★ Cook the pasta following the instructions on the package. Drain.

★ Preheat the oven to 400°F.

★ To make the sauce, melt the 2 tablespoons butter in a saucepan and stir in the flour. Remove from the heat and whisk in the milk a little at a time to make a smooth sauce. Bring to a boil, then reduce the heat and stir until thickened. Remove from the heat and whisk in the Gruyère, a quarter of the Parmesan, and the cream. Season well with salt and pepper and nutmeg.

★ Lightly grease an 8-inch square Pyrex casserole or baking dish. Mix the drained pasta together with the steamed butternut squash and the cheese sauce and spoon into the dish.

★ Mix together the bread crumbs and remaining Parmesan and season with a little salt and pepper. Sprinkle over the pasta and bake in the oven for 20 to 25 minutes, until the top is golden and the sauce is bubbling.

★ Let stand for 15 minutes before serving.

VARIATION: If you like, add some diced cooked chicken to this.

- ☺ SUITABLE FROM 1 YEAR
- ⊌ MAKES 4 PORTIONS
- 🕐 PREPARATION TIME: 12 MINUTES / COOKING TIME: 28 MINUTES
- ❄ SUITABLE FOR FREEZING

- ☺ SUITABLE FROM 1 YEAR
- ⊌ MAKES 4 PORTIONS
- 🕐 PREPARATION TIME: 15 MINUTES / COOKING TIME: 15 MINUTES
- ❄ SAUCE SUITABLE FOR FREEZING

Hidden-vegetable tomato sauce

1 tablespoon olive oil
1 medium onion, chopped
¼ leek, white part only, rinsed and diced
1 garlic clove, crushed
3 tablespoons chopped red bell pepper
⅓ cup chopped carrot
heaping ⅓ cup chopped zucchini
1½ tablespoons ketchup
1½ tablespoons tomato paste
1 teaspoon sugar
one 14-ounce can diced tomatoes
⅔ cup vegetable broth

★ Heat the oil in a saucepan and sauté the onion and leek for about 3 minutes, stirring occasionally, until soft. Add the garlic and sauté for 1 minute. Add the bell pepper, carrot, and zucchini and cook for 3 minutes more, stirring occasionally. Add the ketchup, tomato paste, and sugar and cook, stirring, for about 1 minute. Add the diced tomatoes and broth and simmer, uncovered, for 20 minutes, stirring occasionally.

Tuna, plum tomato, and broccoli pasta

1 tablespoon olive oil
1 medium red onion, finely chopped
1⅓ cups sliced button mushrooms
12 oil-packed sun-dried tomatoes, drained and roughly chopped
1½ to 2 tablespoons balsamic vinegar
one 5-ounce can tuna in oil, drained
4 plum tomatoes, seeded and roughly chopped
2 tablespoons chopped fresh basil
8 ounces fusilli pasta
1 cup small broccoli florets

★ Heat the oil in a deep saucepan; add the red onion and cook for 4 to 5 minutes, until soft. Add the mushrooms and sun-dried tomatoes and sauté over medium heat for another 4 minutes. Turn the heat down, then add the balsamic vinegar, tuna, plum tomatoes, and basil. Turn the heat to very low and keep the sauce warm.

★ Cook the pasta following the instructions on the package, adding the broccoli 3 minutes before the end of the cooking time. Add 3 tablespoons of the pasta water to the sauce, then drain the pasta and broccoli and toss with the sauce.

☺ SUITABLE FROM 1 YEAR

⌣ MAKES 4 PORTIONS

🕐 PREPARATION TIME: 15 MINUTES / COOKING TIME: 20 MINUTES

❄ NOT SUITABLE FOR FREEZING

Fusilli with salmon in a light cheese sauce with spring vegetables

This is a favorite recipe of mine; it's a delicious combination of spring vegetables and tender chunks of salmon. It makes a delicious meal for adults as well. The sauce couldn't be simpler—just stir together the ingredients and heat through.

8 ounces fusilli or rotini pasta
2 tablespoons olive oil
1 medium onion, finely chopped
1 garlic clove, crushed
½ orange bell pepper, seeded and cut into strips
1 cup small broccoli florets
1 medium zucchini, sliced and cut into semicircles
9 ounces salmon fillets, skinned
¾ cup fish broth
⅔ cup crème fraîche or heavy cream
¾ cup vegetable broth
2 large tomatoes, peeled, seeded, and cut into chunks
¾ cup grated Parmesan cheese
salt and freshly ground black pepper

★ Cook the fusilli following the instructions on the package. Drain.

★ Heat the oil in a heavy-bottomed saucepan and sauté the onion and garlic for 3 minutes, stirring occasionally. Add the bell pepper, broccoli, and zucchini and sauté for 6 to 7 minutes, until tender, stirring occasionally.

★ Meanwhile, cut the salmon into chunks, put in a saucepan, cover with the fish broth, and poach over low heat for 3 to 4 minutes, until cooked. Remove from the pan, drain, and set aside.

★ Stir the crème fraîche and vegetable broth into the cooked vegetables and bring to a simmer. Stir in the tomatoes and chunks of salmon and simmer for 2 minutes, then stir in the Parmesan and season to taste with salt and pepper.

★ Toss the drained fusilli with the sauce, taking care not to break up the chunks of salmon.

- SUITABLE FROM 2 YEARS
- MAKES 4 PORTIONS
- PREPARATION TIME: 10 MINUTES / COOKING TIME: 30 MINUTES
- SUITABLE FOR FREEZING

Cod and spinach pasta bake

Cod Florentine, fish cooked with a creamy sauce and spinach, is a wonderful comfort dish. I have taken it one step further by turning this classic into a hearty pasta bake.

8 ounces penne pasta
4 tablespoons (½ stick) butter
5 tablespoons all-purpose flour
2½ cups whole milk
1 teaspoon whole-grain mustard
1 tablespoon chopped fresh dill
1 cup grated Parmesan cheese
salt and freshly ground black
    pepper
8 ounces baby spinach
8 ounces cod, skinned
juice of ½ lemon

★ Preheat the oven to 400°F.
★ Cook the pasta following the instructions on the package. Drain and refresh with cold water. Set aside in the colander.
★ Melt the butter in a saucepan, add the flour, and stir over medium heat for 2 minutes. Add the milk slowly, stirring until combined. Bring to a boil and simmer for 2 minutes, or until it has thickened. Add the mustard, dill, and half the Parmesan. Season well with salt and pepper.
★ Heat 1 tablespoon water in a skillet, add the spinach, and stir over high heat until wilted, then add to the sauce. Mix the penne with the sauce. Cut the cod into ¾-inch cubes and fold into the mixture with the lemon juice.
★ Spoon into an ovenproof dish and sprinkle with the remaining Parmesan. Bake for 20 to 25 minutes, until bubbling and lightly golden on top and the fish is cooked through.

- SUITABLE FROM 19 MONTHS
- MAKES 4 PORTIONS
- PREPARATION TIME: 15 MINUTES (PLUS 30 MINUTES CHILLING) / COOKING TIME: 15 MINUTES
- NOT SUITABLE FOR FREEZING

Salmon and orzo salad

This salad would be great for lunch boxes or picnics as well as a light lunch. The red bell pepper and cucumber add a good crunchy texture and the fresh herbs give the dish a nice summery flavor. Adults love this dish, too!

10 ounces salmon fillet, skinned
a pat of butter
1 heaping cup orzo or other small pasta shapes
1²/₃ cups frozen peas
1 red bell pepper, seeded and diced
½ cucumber, peeled, seeded, and diced
1 small bunch scallions, thinly sliced
2 tablespoons chopped fresh parsley
2 tablespoons chopped fresh dill
2 tablespoons chopped fresh chives
2 tablespoons olive oil
3 tablespoons rice wine vinegar
1 teaspoon honey
salt and freshly ground black pepper

★ Preheat the oven to 350°F.

★ Put the salmon fillet on a piece of aluminum foil on a baking sheet with the butter. Seal the foil to look like a package, then bake in the oven for 15 minutes, or until the salmon is cooked through. Remove from the oven and let cool. Alternatively, you could cut the salmon into chunks, put it into a saucepan, and poach in enough fish broth to cover the fish over medium to low heat for about 7 minutes, or until the fish flakes easily with a fork. Drain and let cool.

★ Cook the pasta following the instructions on the package, and add the peas 4 minutes before the end of the cooking time. Drain and refresh with cold water. Set aside in the colander.

★ Combine the remaining ingredients in a large bowl, seasoning well with the salt and pepper. Carefully stir in the cooked pasta and peas, then flake the salmon and add with any juices from the foil. Cover and chill for 30 minutes before serving.

- SUITABLE FROM 2 YEARS
- MAKES 4 PORTIONS
- PREPARATION TIME: 10 MINUTES / COOKING TIME: 10 MINUTES
- NOT SUITABLE FOR FREEZING

Teriyaki salmon with noodles

Mirin is a sweet Japanese rice wine used in cooking. It is delicious in marinades and dressings. You could also marinate the salmon for half an hour, thread it onto skewers, and broil it for 2 minutes on each side. Oily fish such as salmon provides the best source of essential fatty acids that will help boost your child's brainpower.

TERIYAKI SAUCE
¼ cup mirin
¼ cup soy sauce
1 teaspoon cornstarch
1 tablespoon light brown sugar
1 tablespoon water

4 ounces Chinese egg noodles
   (chow mein noodles)
9 ounces salmon fillet, skinned
salt and freshly ground
   black pepper
2 tablespoons canola oil
2 scallions, chopped
4 ounces sliced sugar snap peas
1¼ cups bean sprouts

★ First, make the sauce: Mix all of the sauce ingredients together in a small bowl.

★ Cook the noodles following the instructions on the package. Drain.

★ Cut the salmon into small cubes and place in a bowl with 2 tablespoons of the sauce. Toss together and season with salt and pepper. Heat 1 tablespoon of the oil in a wok and sauté the salmon for 2 minutes on each side, then carefully transfer to a plate.

★ Heat the remaining 1 tablespoon oil. Stir-fry the scallions and sugar snap peas for 3 minutes. Add the noodles and bean sprouts and stir-fry for 2 minutes. Add the remaining sauce and toss together. Add the salmon and carefully toss together.

Tomato and mascarpone sauce with shrimp

A simple but tasty tomato sauce you could also make without the shrimp if you don't like seafood.

1 tablespoon olive oil
1 medium onion, finely chopped
2 garlic cloves, crushed
1 red chile, seeded and diced
one 14-ounce can diced tomatoes
scant ½ cup mascarpone cheese
8 ounces penne pasta
8 ounces shelled large shrimp, cooked
2 tablespoons finely chopped fresh chives
juice of ½ small lemon

★ Heat the oil in a saucepan and add the onion, garlic, and chile. Cook for 5 minutes over low heat. Add the tomatoes, cover, and simmer for 10 minutes. Add the mascarpone, then whiz in a food processor until smooth.

★ Put back into the saucepan and keep warm while you cook the penne following the instructions on the package. Drain.

★ Add the shrimp and chives to the sauce. Heat through, then add the lemon juice and drained pasta.

Sweet-and-sour meatballs

One of my signature recipes is my chicken-and-apple balls, in which I use grated apple. I also add apple to my meatballs to give them a good flavor and to keep them nice and moist. The sauce is quick and easy to prepare and can be served with pasta or rice.

MEATBALLS
1 tablespoon olive oil
1 medium red onion, chopped
1 garlic clove, crushed
8 ounces lean ground beef
¼ cup grated peeled apple
½ cup fresh bread crumbs
1 tablespoon chopped fresh parsley
2 teaspoons ketchup
salt and freshly ground
   black pepper

8 ounces Chinese egg noodles
   (chow mein noodles)

SAUCE
2 tablespoons soy sauce
¼ cup ketchup
1 tablespoon rice wine vinegar
1 teaspoon light brown sugar
⅔ cup water
2 teaspoons cornstarch mixed with
   a little water

2 scallions, very thinly
   sliced, to serve (optional)

★ Heat 1½ teaspoons of the oil in a large saucepan and sauté the onion for 5 minutes, or until softened but not colored. Add the garlic and sauté for 1 minute, then set aside to cool.
★ Mix the ground beef, apple, bread crumbs, parsley, and ketchup together in a bowl.
★ Add half the cooked onion and garlic to the meat mixture. Season with a little salt and pepper. Shape into 24 small meatballs. Heat the remaining 1½ teaspoons of oil in a skillet. Cook the meatballs over low heat for about 10 minutes, or until golden and cooked through.
★ Cook the noodles following the instructions on the package. Drain.
★ Add the sauce ingredients to the remaining onion and garlic mixture. Bring to a boil and simmer for 2 minutes, or until the sauce has reduced slightly. Mix the sauce with the drained noodles and serve topped with the meatballs and scallions, if using.

☺ SUITABLE FROM 18 MONTHS

🥣 MAKES 4 PORTIONS

🕐 PREPARATION TIME: 15 MINUTES / COOKING TIME: 25 MINUTES

❄ NOT SUITABLE FOR FREEZING

Veal escalopes with tomato and basil sauce

TOMATO SAUCE
3 tablespoons olive oil
1 medium onion, chopped
2 garlic cloves, crushed
two 14-ounce cans diced tomatoes
1 tablespoon tomato paste
1 tablespoon ketchup
1 teaspoon sugar
1 teaspoon fresh thyme or
   ½ teaspoon dried thyme

8 ounces spaghetti
3 tablespoons chopped fresh
   basil leaves

2¾ cups fresh bread crumbs
⅓ cup grated Parmesan cheese
2 tablespoons chopped fresh parsley
4 thin veal escalopes (about
   4 ounces each)
salt and freshly ground black pepper
¼ cup all-purpose flour, for dusting
2 eggs, lightly beaten

★ Heat 1 tablespoon of the olive oil in a saucepan. Add the onion and garlic and sauté for 2 to 3 minutes. Add the canned tomatoes, tomato paste, ketchup, sugar, and thyme. Bring to a boil, cover, and simmer for 20 minutes. Whiz the sauce to a puree using a handheld blender.

★ Cook the pasta following the instructions on the package. Drain and add to the sauce with the basil.

★ Mix together the bread crumbs, Parmesan, and parsley. Spread out on a plate and set aside. If necessary, cover the veal with plastic wrap and pound to a thickness of ⅛ inch using a mallet. Season the veal with salt and pepper, dust with the flour, and dip in the beaten egg. Coat the veal with the bread crumb mixture. Heat the remaining 2 tablespoons oil in a large nonstick skillet. Sauté the veal for 1½ to 2 minutes on both sides, until golden and just cooked through. Remove from the heat and let rest for 2 minutes

★ Spoon some of the spaghetti onto each plate and serve with a veal escalope on top.

SUITABLE FROM 2 YEARS

MAKES 4 PORTIONS

PREPARATION TIME: 5 MINUTES / COOKING TIME: 10 MINUTES

NOT SUITABLE FOR FREEZING

Salami, sweet red pepper, and mozzarella pasta

Most children like salami, so here is a simple recipe that you can put together in about 15 minutes.

6 ounces rotini or fusilli pasta
2 tablespoons olive oil
½ red bell pepper, seeded
    and diced
1 small garlic clove, crushed
2 ounces thinly sliced salami,
    roughly chopped
½ pint cherry tomatoes, each
    tomato cut into 8 pieces
4 ounces fresh mozzarella cheese,
    diced
salt and freshly ground black
    pepper
grated Parmesan cheese, to serve

★ Cook the pasta following the instructions on the package. Drain.
★ Heat the oil in a saucepan. Sauté the bell pepper for 5 minutes, then add the garlic and salami. Sauté for another 5 minutes. Add the drained pasta, cherry tomatoes, and mozzarella and season with salt and pepper. Serve with a little Parmesan cheese sprinkled on top.

SUITABLE FROM 2 YEARS

MAKES 4 PORTIONS

PREPARATION TIME: 10 MINUTES / COOKING TIME: 28 MINUTES

NOT SUITABLE FOR FREEZING

Fusilli with sausage and sweet peppers

You can't go wrong with sausage and pasta. This would be a good dish to make if you had a group of children over, as it is so quick and easy to prepare.

8 ounces fusilli pasta
2 tablespoons olive oil
¾ cup diced onion
1 large garlic clove, chopped
½ each red, yellow, and orange
   bell peppers, seeded and diced
12 ounces of your favorite sausage
1 cup cherry tomatoes, quartered
leaves from 1 small bunch
   of fresh thyme
½ cup grated Cheddar cheese

★ Cook the pasta following the instructions on the package. Drain.

★ Preheat the oven to 400°F.

★ Heat the oil in a saucepan and sauté the onion, garlic, and peppers for 5 minutes. Cook the sausage in the oven or under the broiler. Let cool slightly and cut into chunks.

★ Mix the sausage, drained pasta, bell peppers, tomatoes, and thyme together. Place in a casserole dish and top with the grated cheese. Bake for 20 minutes.

SUITABLE FROM 2 YEARS

MAKES 6 PORTIONS

PREPARATION TIME: 20 MINUTES / COOKING TIME: 1 HOUR 10 MINUTES

SUITABLE FOR FREEZING

Creamy beef cannelloni

This creamy beef cannelloni makes great comfort food. If you like, you can freeze two cannelloni at a time in smaller dishes.

2 tablespoons canola oil

1 large onion, roughly chopped

1 medium carrot, diced

12 ounces lean ground beef

2 garlic cloves, crushed

two 14-ounce cans diced tomatoes

2 tablespoons tomato paste

2 teaspoons sugar

salt and freshly ground black pepper

scant ½ cup heavy cream

small bunch of fresh basil, chopped, or some dried thyme

12 no-preboil cannelloni tubes

½ cup grated Cheddar cheese

★ First, make the filling: Heat 1 tablespoon of the oil in a large saucepan. Add half the onion and all of the carrot and sauté for a few minutes. Add the ground beef and brown over high heat. Add 1 garlic clove, then 1 can of diced tomatoes and 1 tablespoon of the tomato paste. Stir together. Cover and simmer for 30 to 40 minutes, until tender and most of the liquid has been absorbed. Stir in 1 teaspoon of the sugar and season with salt and pepper. Let cool.

★ Preheat the oven to 400°F.

★ Make the creamy tomato sauce: Heat the remaining 1 tablespoon oil in a saucepan. Add the remaining onion and garlic, sweat for a few minutes, then add the remaining can of tomatoes, 1 tablespoon tomato paste, and 1 teaspoon sugar. Cover and simmer for 15 minutes. Add the heavy cream and whiz using a handheld blender until smooth.

★ Spoon a little of the creamy sauce onto the bottom of a small ovenproof dish. Mix the basil into the beef mixture, then stuff the cannelloni tubes with the beef and place in a single layer across the dish. Pour in the remaining sauce and sprinkle with the cheese. Bake for about 30 minutes, or until bubbling and golden on top.

Pork and beef meatballs with tagine sauce

It is important to introduce new flavors to your child, who will often have more sophisticated tastes than you might imagine. Try this mildly spiced Moroccan tagine. It makes a tasty meal that the whole family can enjoy. You can use ground chicken instead of pork.

TAGINE SAUCE
1 tablespoon olive oil
1 small onion, finely chopped
1½ cups coarsely grated peeled butternut squash
½ teaspoon grated fresh ginger
½ teaspoon garam masala
½ teaspoon ground cinnamon
½ teaspoon ground coriander
one 14-ounce can diced tomatoes
1 cup chicken broth
1 teaspoon ketchup
1 teaspoon honey
salt and freshly ground black pepper

MEATBALLS
4 ounces ground pork
4 ounces ground beef
½ cup fresh bread crumbs
2 tablespoons grated Parmesan cheese
½ teaspoon chopped fresh cilantro
1 egg yolk, lightly beaten

8 ounces pasta of your choice

★ First, make the tagine sauce: Heat the oil in a large saucepan and add the onion and butternut squash. Sauté for 5 minutes, then add the spices and sauté for 1 minute. Add the tomatoes, broth, ketchup, and honey. Season with salt and pepper and simmer for 10 minutes, or until the onion and squash are soft. Blend using a handheld blender until smooth.

★ To make the meatballs, put the ground meats, bread crumbs, cheese, cilantro, and egg yolk into a bowl. Season with salt and pepper and mix together; then shape into 20 balls.

★ Bring the sauce to a boil, then carefully drop in the meatballs in a single layer. Cover and simmer for 15 minutes.

★ Meanwhile, cook the pasta following the instructions on the package. Drain.

★ Serve the meatballs and sauce with the drained pasta.

POULTRY
AND
PASTA

🥣 MAKES 5 PORTIONS

🕐 PREPARATION TIME: 15 MINUTES

☉ COOKING TIME: 15 MINUTES

❄ SUITABLE FOR FREEZING

Corn and chicken laksa

Laksa comes from Singapore and Malaysia, where "slurping" your noodles is considered essential!

6 ounces thin Chinese egg noodles
2 teaspoons canola oil
1 small onion, finely chopped
1 garlic clove, crushed
1 tablespoon mild curry paste
    (such as Patak's)
1 tablespoon light brown sugar
one 14-ounce can coconut milk
1 cup chicken broth
2 teaspoons soy sauce
½ teaspoon chopped seeded red
    chile (just a hint; if it is too hot,
    children may be put off)
1 cup canned corn kernels, drained
½ cup frozen peas
1 cup shredded cooked chicken
4 scallions, thinly sliced, plus extra
    to serve (optional)
2 teaspoons lime or lemon juice

TO SERVE
a handful of fresh cilantro leaves
    (optional)
sliced red chiles (optional)
lime quarters (optional)

★ Cook the noodles following the instructions on the package. Drain.

★ Heat the oil in a wok or a large deep skillet and sauté the onion for 5 to 6 minutes, until soft. Add the garlic, curry paste, and brown sugar and cook for 1 minute more; then add the coconut milk, chicken broth, soy sauce, and chopped red chile. Bring to a boil, then drop in the corn, frozen peas, chicken, and scallions. Simmer for 3 minutes, or until everything is hot, then add the lime or lemon juice.

★ Stir in the drained noodles, heat through, and serve. You can put out bowls of cilantro leaves, extra scallions, sliced chiles, and lime quarters so that everyone can help themselves to their favorites.

☕ MAKES 4 PORTIONS

🕐 PREPARATION TIME: 8 MINUTES

☉ COOKING TIME: 10 MINUTES

❄ NOT SUITABLE FOR FREEZING

Annabel's chicken-pasta salad

Pasta salads make a nice change from sandwiches in lunch boxes, and you could prepare the ingredients the night before and mix everything together in the morning. It's also good to have this made up in the fridge for your child to help himself to it after school.

DRESSING

4½ teaspoons balsamic vinegar
½ teaspoon sugar
1 tablespoon soy sauce
2 tablespoons fresh pesto
  (see page 122) or good-quality
  store-bought
2 tablespoons olive oil

6 ounces cooked skinless, boneless
  chicken breast, cut into pieces
6 ounces pasta shells
4 ounces green beans, each bean
  cut into 3 pieces
2 carrots, grated
1 cup canned corn kernels, drained
⅔ cup quartered cherry tomatoes
salt and freshly ground black
  pepper

★ Mix all of the dressing ingredients together in a bowl. Add the chicken, cover, and put in the refrigerator for 20 minutes to marinate.

★ Cook the pasta following the instructions on the package. Add the beans 4 minutes before the end of the cooking time. Drain and refresh with cold water. Allow to drain again.

★ Add the cold pasta and beans to the dressing and chicken along with the carrots, corn, and tomatoes. Toss together and season well with salt and pepper.

VARIATION: For a change, substitute small broccoli or cauliflower florets for the beans.

MAKES 4 PORTIONS

PREPARATION TIME: 40 MINUTES

COOKING TIME: 20 MINUTES

NOT SUITABLE FOR FREEZING

Annabel's chicken pad thai

If your child is fussy, don't just offer food you are sure that he or she will eat, as this can worsen the problem; keep trying new recipes. This tasty pad thai is usually very popular. You could make this vegetarian by replacing the chicken with more vegetables.

MARINADE
¼ cup mirin
5 tablespoons soy sauce
4½ teaspoons honey

8 ounces skinless, boneless chicken
   breast, thinly sliced
6 ounces medium (pad thai) rice
   noodles
1½ cups small broccoli florets
3 tablespoons canola oil
2 eggs, lightly beaten
1 medium onion, thinly sliced
1 red chile, seeded and thinly sliced
   (optional)
2 garlic cloves, crushed
1 cup snow peas, cut into thin strips
1 small carrot, cut into thin strips
1¼ cups bean sprouts
1½ teaspoons fish sauce (nam pla)

★ Mix together the mirin, soy sauce, and honey in a bowl. Add the chicken, toss to coat, then cover and refrigerate for 30 minutes.
★ Meanwhile, cook the noodles following the instructions on the package, adding the broccoli 3 minutes before the end of the cooking time. Drain in a colander, rinse with cold water, and set aside.
★ Heat 1 tablespoon of the oil in a wok. Add the eggs and cook for 2 to 3 minutes, until set into a thin omelet. Remove the omelet and cut into thin strips. Set aside.
★ Remove the chicken from the marinade, reserving the marinade. Heat 1 tablespoon of the oil in the wok and stir-fry the chicken for 3 to 4 minutes, or until just cooked through. Transfer the chicken to a plate and set aside.
★ Heat the remaining 1 tablespoon oil in the wok and cook the onion for 5 minutes, or until soft. Add the chile, if using, and garlic and cook for 2 minutes. Add the snow peas, carrot, and bean sprouts and cook for 3 minutes, until the vegetables have softened slightly, then add the reserved marinade and bring to a boil. Boil for 10 seconds.
★ Add the cooked chicken, noodles, broccoli, and omelet and toss together over high heat for 2 to 3 minutes, until everything is hot. Add the fish sauce and serve.

MAKES 4 PORTIONS

PREPARATION TIME: 8 MINUTES

COOKING TIME: 10 MINUTES

NOT SUITABLE FOR FREEZING

Fusilli with chicken and pesto

Pesto has a flavor that tends to be popular with children. It is easy to make your own pesto. Simply toast ⅓ cup pine nuts in a dry skillet until golden, then let cool. Put ⅔ cup grated Parmesan cheese, 1 garlic clove, a small bunch of fresh basil, the cooled pine nuts, and a pinch of sugar in a food processor and slowly add some olive oil while the motor is running. Finish with a little water and some salt and pepper.

8 ounces fusilli pasta
a generous pat of butter
1½ cups halved cherry tomatoes
1½ teaspoons olive oil
1 medium onion, sliced
1 garlic clove, crushed
7 ounces skinless, boneless chicken breast, thinly sliced
1 tablespoon balsamic vinegar
1 tablespoon soy sauce
1½ teaspoons lemon juice
2 tablespoons fresh pesto (see headnote or page 122) or good-quality store-bought
6 fresh basil leaves
salt and freshly ground black pepper

★ Cook the pasta following the instructions on the package. Drain.
★ Heat the butter in a small saucepan and sauté the cherry tomatoes for 1 minute, then transfer to a small bowl and set aside.
★ Heat the oil in a wok and sauté the onion and garlic for 3 minutes, stirring occasionally, then add the chicken and continue to stir for 3 minutes, or until the chicken is cooked through. Add the balsamic vinegar, soy sauce, lemon juice, and pesto and cook for 1 minute.
★ Add the drained pasta to the onion and chicken mixture and mix in the sautéed cherry tomatoes and the basil leaves; cook for 1 minute. Season with a little salt and pepper and serve.

Chicken stir-fry with peanut butter sauce

Stir-fries are quick and easy to prepare and a good way to get your child to eat more vegetables if you mix them with a tasty sauce like this peanut butter one.

PEANUT BUTTER SAUCE
2 tablespoons creamy peanut butter
2 teaspoons light brown sugar
1 tablespoon soy sauce
⅔ cup chicken broth
2 teaspoons rice wine vinegar

2 tablespoons olive oil
1 large skinless, boneless chicken breast, cut into thin strips
salt and freshly ground black pepper
1 small onion, thinly sliced
1 garlic clove, crushed
½ red chile, diced
1½ cups small broccoli florets
1 red bell pepper, seeded and cut into thin strips
6 ounces medium (pad thai) rice noodles or rice sticks
2 teaspoons lime juice

★ First, make the sauce: Mix all of the sauce ingredients together in a small bowl and set aside.

★ Heat 1 tablespoon of the oil in a wok or skillet. Season the chicken with salt and pepper, then quickly brown over high heat and place on a plate.

★ Heat the remaining 1 tablespoon oil. Add the onion, garlic, and chile. Sauté over medium heat for 3 to 4 minutes. Add the broccoli and bell pepper and stir-fry for 4 to 5 minutes, until the broccoli is nearly cooked. Return the chicken to the pan along with the sauce. Bring to a boil and season with salt and pepper. Reduce the heat to low and keep warm.

★ Cook the noodles in boiling salted water following the instructions on the package, drain, and add to the wok with the lime juice. Toss everything together and place in a serving dish.

- MAKES 4 PORTIONS
- PREPARATION TIME: 20 MINUTES
- COOKING TIME: 50 MINUTES
- SUITABLE FOR FREEZING

Chicken cannelloni

There are so many things that you can stuff inside cannelloni tubes, such as spinach and ricotta or a meat sauce, but here's something a little different—tasty ground chicken with tomatoes covered with a creamy cheese sauce and a golden topping.

1 tablespoon olive oil
1 medium onion, chopped
1 small garlic clove, crushed
½ cup chopped cremini
    mushrooms
½ teaspoon dried mixed herbs
8 ounces ground chicken
half a 14-ounce can diced tomatoes
1½ teaspoons ketchup

CHEESE SAUCE
2 tablespoons butter
3 tablespoons all-purpose flour
½ teaspoon paprika
1⅔ cups whole milk
1 cup grated Cheddar cheese

8 no-preboil cannelloni tubes

★ Heat the oil in a saucepan and sauté the onion and garlic for 2 minutes. Add the mushrooms, herbs, and chicken and sauté for 3 minutes. Stir in the diced tomatoes and ketchup and simmer for 20 minutes.

★ Preheat the oven to 350°F.

★ Make the cheese sauce: Melt the butter in a saucepan, then stir in the flour and paprika and cook for 1 minute. Gradually whisk in the milk. Bring to a boil and then simmer, stirring, until thickened. Stir in ½ cup of the grated Cheddar.

★ Stuff the cannelloni tubes with the chicken filling. Spoon a little of the cheese sauce onto the bottom of a shallow ovenproof dish, then arrange the cannelloni in the dish. Pour on the cheese sauce, sprinkle with the remaining Cheddar cheese, and bake in the oven for 25 minutes, until golden and bubbling on top.

⊌ MAKES 4 PORTIONS

🕐 PREPARATION TIME: 12 MINUTES

☉ COOKING TIME: 20 MINUTES

❄ NOT SUITABLE FOR FREEZING

Duck confit and tomato ragù rigatoni

Duck confit is cooked and preserved duck legs, which you can buy canned in some delis, gourmet stores, or online. It's very tasty and easy to use.

6 ounces rigatoni pasta
6 ounces duck confit
2 tablespoons olive oil
⅔ cup diced onion
2 garlic cloves, chopped
1¼ pounds tomatoes, chopped
2 sprigs fresh oregano, chopped
salt and freshly ground black
  pepper

★ Preheat the oven to 325°F.
★ Cook the rigatoni following the instructions on the package. Drain.
★ Flake the duck meat off the duck legs and warm the meat in the oven for 15 to 20 minutes.
★ Heat the oil in a saucepan and sauté the onion and garlic for 5 minutes. Add the chopped tomatoes and simmer for 10 minutes. Fold in the duck and oregano. Season to taste with salt and pepper
★ Serve the sauce with the drained pasta.

Singapore noodles

Children often have more adventurous tastes than we might imagine, and I find that they enjoy Asian-style recipes like these noodles, particularly if you give them "child-friendly" chopsticks that are joined at the top to eat with.

MARINADE
2 teaspoons soy sauce
2 teaspoons sake
1½ teaspoons sugar
1½ teaspoons cornstarch

7 ounces skinless, boneless chicken breast, cut into strips
4 ounces thin Chinese egg noodles
2 tablespoons vegetable oil
2 medium carrots, cut into matchsticks
1 garlic clove, crushed
½ red chile, seeded and thinly sliced
1 heaping tablespoon mild korma curry paste (such as Patak's)
⅓ cup coconut milk
¼ cup strong chicken broth (made with half an organic bouillon cube)
4 drops fish sauce
½ cup frozen peas
⅓ cup canned corn kernels, drained

★ Mix together the ingredients for the marinade and marinate the chicken, covered, in the refrigerator for about 30 minutes.
★ Cook the noodles following the instructions on the package. Drain.
★ Heat the oil in a wok and stir-fry the carrots for 4 minutes. Add the garlic and chile and stir-fry for 30 seconds. Add the chicken and stir-fry until just cooked. Stir in the korma curry paste, coconut milk, chicken broth, and fish sauce. Then stir in the peas and corn and cook for about 3 minutes, or until both the chicken and the peas are cooked. Stir in the drained noodles and cook for 2 minutes, or until the noodles are heated through.

MAKES 4 PORTIONS

PREPARATION TIME: 15 MINUTES, PLUS 1 HOUR MARINATING

COOKING TIME: 25 MINUTES

NOT SUITABLE FOR FREEZING

Annabel's pasta salad with marinated chicken and roasted sweet peppers

This is one of my favorite salads. Roasting bell peppers in the oven gives them a deliciously sweet flavor. You could marinate 2 uncooked chicken breasts for about 10 minutes in some olive oil, rice wine vinegar, and pesto, then grill the chicken and serve this as a warm salad.

1 red bell pepper, cut in half and seeded

1 yellow bell pepper, cut in half and seeded

6 ounces rotini or fusilli pasta

2 teaspoons Dijon mustard

¼ cup olive oil

3 tablespoons rice wine vinegar

1 tablespoon fresh pesto (see page 122) or good-quality store-bought

12 ounces cooked chicken breast, cut into thin slices

2 tablespoons chopped fresh parsley

2 scallions, thinly sliced

½ garlic clove, crushed

2 cups lightly packed pea shoots or watercress

salt and freshly ground black pepper

★ Preheat the oven to 400°F.

★ Place the red and yellow bell peppers, cut side down, on a baking sheet. Roast in the oven for 20 to 25 minutes, until soft and the skins are dark brown. Remove from the oven, place in a bowl, cover with plastic wrap, and let cool. Once cool enough to handle, remove the skins and cut the flesh into thin strips.

★ Meanwhile, cook the pasta following the instructions on the package. Drain, rinse with cold water, and let stand in a colander for 10 minutes.

★ Mix together the Dijon mustard, oil, rice wine vinegar, and pesto in a large bowl. Add the chicken, parsley, scallions, garlic, and cooked pasta and toss together along with the roasted peppers. Let marinate in the refrigerator for 1 hour.

★ Scatter a few of the pea shoots or some of the watercress on the bottom of a serving plate. Roughly chop the remaining leaves and fold into the salad with some salt and pepper. Spoon the salad onto the serving plate.

MAKES 4 PORTIONS

PREPARATION TIME: 20 MINUTES

COOKING TIME: 18 MINUTES

NOT SUITABLE FOR FREEZING

Chicken-noodle salad with peanut dressing

This delicious peanut dressing combines well with shredded chicken, rice noodles, and crunchy vegetables.

2 cups chicken broth
2 large chicken thighs
4 ounces thin rice noodles
   (rice vermicelli)
vegetable oil, for tossing
¼ napa cabbage, finely shredded
1 medium carrot, cut into
   matchsticks
¼ English cucumber, peeled and
   cut into matchsticks
4 scallions, sliced

DRESSING
3 tablespoons creamy peanut
   butter
1 tablespoon sweet red chili sauce
¼ cup chicken broth (from
   the poached chicken)
2 tablespoons rice wine vinegar
½ teaspoon superfine sugar
1 tablespoon vegetable oil

★ Bring the chicken broth to a boil in a large saucepan, add the chicken thighs, cover, and simmer for 15 minutes. Lift out the chicken with a slotted spoon and set aside to cool.
★ Return the broth to a boil, turn off the heat, and add the rice noodles. Let soak for about 4 minutes, or until tender, then drain, reserving the chicken broth for the dressing. Rinse the noodles under the tap, and drain. Transfer to a large bowl and toss with a little oil.
★ Remove the skin from the chicken thighs and shred the flesh. Add the shredded chicken to the noodles together with the shredded napa cabbage, the carrot, cucumber, and scallions.
★ Mix together all the ingredients for the dressing and toss with the salad.

- MAKES 6 PORTIONS
- PREPARATION TIME: 12 MINUTES
- COOKING TIME: 40 MINUTES
- SUITABLE FOR FREEZING

Turkey pasta bake with creamy Parmesan and tomato sauce

This is a wonderful recipe for using up leftover roast turkey or chicken. Turkey and penne are mixed together with a tasty tomato sauce made from sweet peppers and sun-dried tomatoes, and covered in a creamy Parmesan sauce.

8 ounces penne pasta

TOMATO SAUCE
2 tablespoons olive oil
1 medium onion, chopped
1 red bell pepper, seeded and diced
1 garlic clove, crushed
one 14-ounce can diced tomatoes
2 teaspoons balsamic vinegar
1 tablespoon tomato paste
2 tablespoons chopped fresh basil
10 oil-packed sun-dried tomatoes,
    roughly chopped
1 teaspoon dried oregano
8 ounces cooked turkey or
    chicken, cut into strips

PARMESAN SAUCE
3 tablespoons butter
¼ cup all-purpose flour
1⅔ cups hot chicken broth
½ cup heavy cream
1 cup grated Parmesan cheese

★ Preheat the oven to 350°F.
★ Cook the penne following the instructions on the package. Drain and refresh with cold water. Drain again.
★ Make the tomato sauce: Heat the oil in a saucepan. Add the onion, bell pepper, and garlic and simmer for 8 minutes, or until just tender. Add the diced tomatoes, vinegar, and tomato paste and simmer for 5 minutes. Add the basil, sun-dried tomatoes, and oregano, then the turkey or chicken and the penne. Mix together, then spoon into a shallow ovenproof dish.
★ Make the Parmesan sauce: Melt the butter in a saucepan. Add the flour and stir over low heat for 1 minute. Add the broth, slowly stirring until thickened. Stir in the cream and ½ cup of the Parmesan. Spoon over the pasta and sprinkle the remaining Parmesan on top.
★ Bake for 15 to 20 minutes, until hot, then finish off under a preheated broiler for about 3 minutes, or until golden.

Caesar salad with chicken, pasta, and crispy bacon

Caesar salad is a classic favorite, but to give it more child appeal, why not add some pasta? Some children are not keen on avocado (I think they don't like the mushy texture), so if your child doesn't like it, leave it out.

6 ounces farfalle (bow tie) pasta

DRESSING
2 teaspoons Dijon mustard
1 tablespoon white wine vinegar
1 small garlic clove, crushed
2 tablespoons lemon juice
⅓ cup light mayonnaise
⅓ cup cold water
½ teaspoon Worcestershire sauce
⅓ cup grated Parmesan cheese
salt and freshly ground black pepper

SALAD
1⅓ cups diced cooked chicken breast
⅓ cup halved cherry tomatoes
1 small avocado, cut into cubes
2 tablespoons chopped fresh chives
½ cup coarsely grated Parmesan cheese
6 ounces crispy cooked bacon, roughly chopped

★ Cook the pasta following the instructions on the package. Drain, rinse with cold water, and let stand in a colander for 10 minutes.
★ Make the dressing: Measure the mustard, vinegar, garlic, and lemon juice into a small bowl. Whisk together, then add the mayonnaise, water, Worcestershire sauce, and cheese and whisk until smooth. Season to taste with salt and pepper.
★ Mix the pasta and all of the salad ingredients together in a large bowl. Spoon the dressing over and mix together.

🥣 MAKES 4 PORTIONS

🕐 PREPARATION TIME: 15 MINUTES

☉ COOKING TIME: 25 MINUTES

❋ NOT SUITABLE FOR FREEZING

Pasta pesto chicken with Parma ham

Tender chicken breasts with mozzarella and pesto are wrapped in Parma ham and served on a bed of curly pasta shapes. This is a delicious family dish that would also make a stunning entrée for a special supper party.

8 ounces fresh mozzarella cheese

3 to 4 tablespoons fresh pesto (see page 122) or good-quality store-bought

4 small skinless, boneless chicken breasts

a bunch of fresh basil

4 slices Parma ham

1 cup cherry tomatoes

1 tablespoon honey

8 ounces chifferi rigati pasta, elbows, or similar short pasta

1 tablespoon olive oil

1 medium onion

2 garlic cloves, crushed

¼ cup crème fraîche or heavy cream

1 tablespoon lemon juice

★ Preheat the oven to 400°F.

★ Cut the mozzarella into 8 thin slices. Spread 1 teaspoon pesto over each chicken breast. Put 2 slices of mozzarella on top and 1 basil leaf. Wrap each breast in 1 slice of Parma ham. Arrange on a baking sheet. Put the tomatoes around the chicken. Drizzle the honey over the ham. Bake for 20 to 25 minutes, or until the ham is crisp and the chicken is cooked through.

★ Meanwhile, cook the pasta following the instructions on the package. Drain.

★ Heat the oil in a saucepan, add the onion and garlic, and sauté for 4 to 5 minutes, until soft. Add the pasta, crème fraîche, and lemon juice, then roughly tear the remaining basil leaves and add. Stir in 2 tablespoons pesto. Spoon some pasta onto each plate. Place a chicken breast on top and garnish with the tomatoes.

Fusilli with chicken and spring vegetables

Using a combination of sun-dried and fresh tomatoes gives this sauce extra flavor. Some delis sell oven-roasted tomatoes, which are softer and moister than sun-dried tomatoes, and those would be really good in this dish, too.

1 tablespoon olive oil
1 medium red onion, chopped
1 red bell pepper, seeded and diced
3 ounces pancetta, roughly chopped
1 large skinless, boneless chicken
   breast, cut into thin strips
4 large tomatoes, seeded
   and roughly chopped
12 oil-packed sun-dried tomatoes,
   roughly chopped
¼ cup crème fraîche or heavy cream
8 ounces fusilli pasta
¾ cup frozen peas

★ Heat the oil in a skillet, add the onion and bell pepper, and sauté for 4 minutes, or until just starting to soften. Add the pancetta and chicken and sauté until the chicken is cooked and the pancetta is crispy. Turn down the heat, then add the fresh tomatoes, sun-dried tomatoes, and crème fraîche.

★ Cook the pasta following the instructions on the package. Add the peas 3 minutes before the end of the cooking time. Add 3 tablespoons of the pasta water to the sauce before draining the pasta and tossing it in the sauce.

MAKES 4 PORTIONS

PREPARATION TIME: 15 MINUTES

COOKING TIME: 20 MINUTES

NOT SUITABLE FOR FREEZING

Open chicken-and-broccoli lasagne

2 large skinless, boneless chicken
  breasts
1 garlic clove, crushed
1 tablespoon olive oil
1 sprig fresh thyme

CHEESE SAUCE
2 tablespoons butter
2 tablespoons all-purpose flour
1¼ cups whole milk
½ cup grated sharp Cheddar cheese
½ cup grated Gruyère cheese
⅓ cup grated Parmesan cheese
½ teaspoon Dijon mustard
a little grated nutmeg
salt and freshly ground
  black pepper

oil, for greasing
1½ cups small broccoli florets
6 sheets fresh lasagne (about
  6 ounces; thawed if frozen)

★ Cut the chicken breasts in half horizontally. Mix together the garlic, oil, and thyme and rub over the chicken. Allow to marinate for 10 minutes while you make the cheese sauce.

★ To make the cheese sauce, melt the butter, stir in the flour, and cook for 1 minute. Gradually stir in the milk. Bring to a boil and cook, stirring constantly, over medium heat, until the sauce thickens enough to coat the back of a spoon. Remove from the heat and stir in the Cheddar, Gruyère, half the Parmesan, and the mustard. Add a little nutmeg and season to taste with salt and pepper. Keep warm.

★ Heat a grill pan and brush with oil. Season the chicken with salt and pepper and grill for 3 to 4 minutes on each side, until cooked through. Alternatively, stir-fry the chicken (cut the breasts into thin slices instead of in half).

★ Cook the broccoli in boiling salted water, or steam, for 4 minutes, or until tender. Drain. Blanch the lasagne sheets in boiling salted water. Drain, and cut each sheet in half.

★ Preheat the broiler.

★ Assemble the lasagne on 4 heatproof plates. Put 1 square of pasta on each plate. Slice the chicken and divide half of it among the plates, along with half of the broccoli and one-third of the cheese sauce. Repeat with another layer of pasta, chicken, broccoli, and sauce. Top with a square of pasta and spoon the remaining sauce on top. Sprinkle with the remaining Parmesan and broil each one for 2 to 3 minutes to heat slightly and brown the Parmesan.

★ Serve immediately.

Marinated chicken stir-fry with pasta

A simple and quick dish of chicken marinated in soy sauce and sake (a sweet Japanese rice wine), stir-fried with a selection of vegetables, then finished off with a tasty combination of soy, plum, and oyster sauces.

MARINADE
1 tablespoon soy sauce
1 tablespoon sake
1 teaspoon Asian sesame oil
1 teaspoon cornstarch
½ teaspoon sugar

1 large skinless, boneless chicken breast, cut into thin strips
4 ounces farfalle (bow tie) pasta
2 teaspoons Asian sesame oil
½ medium onion, sliced
1 red bell pepper, seeded and sliced

STIR-FRY SAUCE
1 tablespoon soy sauce
1 tablespoon plum sauce
1 tablespoon oyster sauce
⅔ cup chicken broth
2 teaspoons cornstarch

⅔ cup small broccoli florets
4 scallions, sliced
4 ounces bean sprouts

★ Measure all of the marinade ingredients into a bowl and add the chicken. Toss together, then cover and allow to marinate in the refrigerator for 30 minutes.

★ Meanwhile, cook the pasta following the instructions on the package. Drain.

★ Heat the 2 teaspoons sesame oil in a wok. Add the onion and bell pepper and stir-fry for 2 minutes. Add the chicken and marinade and stir-fry for 2 minutes.

★ Mix together all of the sauce ingredients, then pour over the chicken. Add the broccoli, cooked pasta, and scallions and simmer for 4 minutes. Add the bean sprouts. Toss together and serve at once.

Honey and mustard chicken with sweet pepper

Mild whole-grain mustard and honey add a delicious flavor to the marinated chicken.

2 large skinless, boneless chicken breasts, cut into thin strips
1 teaspoon paprika
2 teaspoons whole-grain mustard
2 teaspoons honey
1 tablespoon Worcestershire sauce
2 tablespoons canola oil
salt and freshly ground black pepper
1 small onion, finely chopped
1 yellow bell pepper, seeded and diced
⅓ cup chicken broth
⅔ cup crème fraîche or heavy cream
⅔ cup halved cherry tomatoes
pinch of sugar

4 ounces penne pasta
chopped fresh parsley, to serve

★ Put the chicken strips into a bowl. Measure the paprika, mustard, honey, and Worcestershire sauce on top and toss together. Cover and allow to marinate in the refrigerator for 30 minutes.

★ Heat 1 tablespoon of the oil in a nonstick skillet. Season the chicken with salt and pepper, then quickly brown it and transfer to a plate.

★ Heat the remaining 1 tablespoon oil. Add the onion and bell pepper and sauté for 4 to 5 minutes, until very soft. Add any remaining marinade from the bowl to the pan. Add the broth, bring to a boil, then stir in the crème fraîche. Return the chicken to the pan and simmer for 5 minutes, or until cooked through. Just before serving, stir in the cherry tomatoes and sugar.

★ Meanwhile, cook the penne following the instructions on the package. Drain.

★ Serve the chicken and sauce with the penne and chopped parsley.

MEATY
MENUS

- MAKES 12 PORTIONS
- PREPARATION TIME: 12 MINUTES
- COOKING TIME: 40 MINUTES
- SUITABLE FOR FREEZING

Bolognese gratin

This could also be served without the cheese as a regular spaghetti bolognese.

2 tablespoons olive oil
1 medium red onion, finely chopped
½ red bell pepper, seeded and
   diced
1 medium carrot, diced
½ celery stalk, finely chopped
⅔ cup chopped zucchini
⅓ cup grated peeled apple
1 garlic clove, crushed
one 14-ounce can diced tomatoes
½ cup beef broth
1 pound lean ground beef
2 tablespoons tomato paste
3 tablespoons ketchup
½ teaspoon dried thyme
¼ teaspoon freshly ground black
   pepper, plus extra to taste
salt

8 ounces rotini or fusilli pasta
½ cup grated Cheddar cheese

★ Heat the oil in a large saucepan and sauté the vegetables and apple for 10 to 15 minutes, stirring frequently, until soft and slightly colored, then add the garlic and cook for 1 minute. Transfer to a blender, add the tomatoes and broth, and whiz until smooth. Return to the pan.

★ Brown the ground beef in a nonstick skillet (you don't need any oil) and add to the vegetable-and-tomato mixture in the saucepan along with the tomato paste, ketchup, thyme, and the ¼ teaspoon black pepper. Mix together, bring to a boil, and simmer for 20 to 25 minutes. Season to taste with salt and, if desired, the extra pepper.

★ Meanwhile, cook the pasta following the instructions on the package. Drain, and mix with the sauce.

★ Preheat the broiler.

★ Place the pasta and sauce in a large baking dish, sprinkle with the cheese, and brown under the broiler.

- MAKES 24 MEATBALLS/ 4 TO 6 PORTIONS
- PREPARATION TIME: 20 MINUTES
- COOKING TIME: 30 MINUTES
- SUITABLE FOR FREEZING

Italian meatballs with penne and tomato sauce

These meatballs in tomato sauce are perfect for freezing in individual portions.

MEATBALLS
8 ounces lean ground beef
2 teaspoons fresh pesto
   (see page 122) or good-quality
   store-bought
½ cup grated peeled apple
½ cup fresh bread crumbs
½ small garlic clove, crushed
3 tablespoons grated Parmesan
   cheese
2 teaspoons chopped fresh basil
1 egg yolk, lightly beaten

TOMATO SAUCE
1 tablespoon olive oil
1 medium onion, chopped
½ garlic clove, crushed
two 14-ounce cans diced tomatoes
2 teaspoons sugar
½ teaspoon balsamic vinegar
1 tablespoon tomato paste
salt and freshly ground black pepper

6 ounces penne pasta
2 tablespoons chopped fresh basil
   (optional)

★ First, make the meatballs: Put all the meatball ingredients into a bowl, mix together using your hands, and form into 24 mini meatballs. Put in the refrigerator while you make the sauce.

★ Heat the oil in a large saucepan and sauté the onion and garlic for 2 to 3 minutes, until soft. Add the tomatoes, sugar, balsamic vinegar, and tomato paste. Bring to a boil, then simmer, uncovered, for 10 to 15 minutes, until the sauce has reduced and thickened slightly. Season with a little salt and pepper.

★ Add the meatballs, coat them in the tomato sauce, cover, and simmer for 10 to 12 minutes, until the meatballs are cooked through.

★ Cook the pasta following the instructions on the package. Drain.

★ Mix the pasta and sauce together and sprinkle with the basil, if you wish (although some children don't like to see green bits in the sauce).

◔ MAKES 4 PORTIONS

⏰ PREPARATION TIME: 15 MINUTES

☉ COOKING TIME: 25 MINUTES

❄ SUITABLE FOR FREEZING (STROGANOFF ONLY)

Beef stroganoff with tagliatelle

I buy the narrow end of a beef tenderloin from my butcher to make stroganoff; it's sometimes cheaper than normal filet mignon and tastes the same, so it's perfect. Traditionally, you make this with button mushrooms, but cremini mushrooms are also good, or if you are feeling extravagant, you could use fresh shiitake mushrooms.

1 to 2 tablespoons olive oil
2 cups thinly sliced mushrooms
8 ounces top loin (strip) steak or
   beef tenderloin, thinly sliced
a large pat of butter
3 small shallots, thinly sliced
1 garlic clove, crushed
½ teaspoon fresh thyme leaves
1¼ cups beef broth
¾ cup heavy cream
½ teaspoon Dijon mustard
2 teaspoons soy sauce
1 teaspoon sugar
freshly ground black pepper
a small squeeze of lemon juice
8 ounces tagliatelle
chopped fresh parsley, to serve

★ Heat 2 teaspoons of the oil in a wok or a large skillet. Sauté the mushrooms for 5 to 6 minutes, until golden brown. Transfer to a bowl. Heat another teaspoon of oil in the pan and sauté the steak quickly (1 to 2 minutes) until browned. Don't overcrowd the pan—it is best to cook the meat in 2 or 3 batches (with a little extra oil) to prevent stewing the beef in its own juices. Transfer the beef to the bowl with the mushrooms.

★ Turn the heat down to low. Melt the butter and gently cook the shallots for 8 to 10 minutes, until soft. Add the garlic and thyme and cook for 1 minute. Add the beef broth, bring to a boil, and boil for 2 to 3 minutes, until reduced by half. Whisk in the cream, mustard, soy sauce, and sugar and boil for 2 to 3 minutes, until thick enough to coat the back of a spoon. Reduce the heat to low and add the mushrooms and beef. Season with black pepper and the lemon juice (you probably won't need to add salt).

★ Cook the tagliatelle following the instructions on the package. Drain, and transfer to plates. Spoon the stroganoff over the tagliatelle. Serve sprinkled with parsley.

⊌ MAKES 4 PORTIONS

🕐 PREPARATION TIME: 20 MINUTES

◉ COOKING TIME: 40 MINUTES

❄ SUITABLE FOR FREEZING (WITHOUT THE MOZZARELLA)

Mozzarella and meatball pasta bake

Like strawberries and cream, pesto and mozzarella are great partners.

8 ounces fusilli pasta

SAUCE
1 tablespoon olive oil
1 large red onion, chopped
2 garlic cloves, crushed
two 14-ounce cans diced tomatoes
1 tablespoon tomato paste
1 teaspoon sugar
3 tablespoons chopped fresh basil

MEATBALLS
8 ounces lean ground beef
3 tablespoons fresh pesto (see page 122) or good-quality store-bought
1 cup fresh bread crumbs
½ cup grated Parmesan cheese
1 egg yolk
salt and freshly ground black pepper
canola oil, for browning

8 ounces fresh mozzarella cheese, diced

★ Preheat the oven to 400°F.
★ Cook the pasta following the instructions on the package until just cooked. Drain and refresh with cold water. Set aside in the colander.
★ Heat the oil in a saucepan and add the onion and garlic. Cook for 5 minutes over low heat, then add the tomatoes. Bring to a boil, then simmer, uncovered, for 15 minutes, or until the sauce has reduced and thickened. Add the tomato paste and sugar and stir in the basil.
★ Mix the ground beef with 1 tablespoon of the pesto, the bread crumbs, ¼ cup of the Parmesan, the egg yolk, and salt and pepper. Shape the meat mixture into 24 small balls. Heat a thin layer of oil in a nonstick skillet and brown the meatballs.
★ Mix together the pasta, tomato sauce, half the mozzarella, and all the meatballs, then spoon into an ovenproof dish. Blob the remaining 2 tablespoons pesto over the pasta. Sprinkle with the remaining mozzarella and Parmesan. Bake for 20 to 25 minutes, until golden brown and heated through.

⊌ MAKES 4 PORTIONS

⏱ PREPARATION TIME: 8 MINUTES

☉ COOKING TIME: 12 MINUTES

❋ SUITABLE FOR FREEZING

⊌ MAKES 4 PORTIONS

⏱ PREPARATION TIME: 5 MINUTES

☉ COOKING TIME: 10 MINUTES

❋ NOT SUITABLE FOR FREEZING

Sausage, sage, and red onion fusilli

6 ounces fusilli pasta
2 tablespoons canola oil
2 large red onions, thinly sliced
1 tablespoon honey
2 tablespoons light brown sugar
1 pound of your favorite sausage
10 fresh sage leaves
salt and freshly ground black pepper

★ Cook the fusilli following the instructions on the package. Drain.
★ Heat the oil in a saucepan and sauté the onions until soft. Add the honey and brown sugar and cook for 10 minutes, stirring frequently, until caramelized.
★ Cook the sausage in a nonstick skillet or under the broiler for 6 to 10 minutes, until cooked through, then cut them into pieces. Chop the sage leaves. Mix together the drained pasta, caramelized onion, sausage, and sage leaves. Season to taste with salt and pepper and serve.

Penne carbonara

1 tablespoon canola oil
6 ounces bacon or pancetta, diced
8 ounces penne pasta
½ cup heavy cream
½ cup chicken broth
⅓ cup grated Parmesan cheese, plus extra for serving
1 egg yolk
salt and freshly ground pepper

★ Heat the oil in a skillet and fry the bacon for 5 to 8 minutes, until crisp. Drain on paper towels.
★ Cook the pasta following the instructions on the package. Meanwhile, put the cream, broth, ⅓ cup Parmesan, and the egg yolk into a bowl and whisk together.
★ Drain the pasta and return it to the pot. Add the sauce mixture and the bacon and cook over low heat, stirring constantly, for 2 to 3 minutes, until the sauce is hot and has thickened. Season with salt and pepper. Serve with extra Parmesan.

- MAKES 4 TO 6 PORTIONS
- PREPARATION TIME: 10 MINUTES
- COOKING TIME: 45 MINUTES
- SUITABLE FOR FREEZING (SAUCE ONLY)

Spaghetti bolognese with pesto

Spaghetti bolognese is always a crowd-pleaser, and this has a bit of a twist, as I add some chopped sun-dried tomatoes and pesto.

2 tablespoons olive oil
⅓ cup chopped onion
⅓ cup diced leek
2 garlic cloves, finely chopped
1¼ pounds lean ground beef
½ cup beef broth
2 tomatoes, seeded and diced
one 14-ounce can diced tomatoes
12 oil-packed sun-dried tomatoes, roughly chopped
12 ounces spaghetti
2 tablespoons fresh pesto (see page 122) or good quality store-bought
salt and freshly ground black pepper

★ Heat the oil in a large saucepan. Sauté the onion and leek for about 5 minutes, until softened but not colored. Add the garlic and cook for 1 minute. Add the ground beef and sauté, stirring occasionally, until browned. Stir in the broth and the fresh, canned, and sun-dried tomatoes. Simmer for 35 to 40 minutes, until thickened.

★ Meanwhile, cook the spaghetti following the instructions on the package. Drain.

★ Stir the pesto into the sauce, season to taste with salt and pepper, and toss the sauce with the pasta.

🥣 MAKES 4 PORTIONS

🕐 PREPARATION TIME: 12 MINUTES

☉ COOKING TIME: 12 MINUTES

❄ IF YOU FREEZE THE BEEF FOR 1 HOUR, IT WILL MAKE SLICING EASIER.

Stir-fried beef with noodles

This is one of my favorite recipes, which is also loved by my children and often requested by them when I ask what they would like for supper. This sauce has a lovely rich Japanese-style flavor.

12 ounces top loin (strip), sirloin, or filet mignon steak
2 eggs
¼ cup plus 1 teaspoon cornstarch
a pinch of salt
1 medium carrot
2 medium zucchini, peeled
3 tablespoons rice wine vinegar
2 tablespoons soy sauce
3 tablespoons chicken broth or water
canola oil
4 scallions, sliced
1 red chile, seeded and chopped
1 garlic clove, crushed
4 ounces medium Chinese egg noodles (chow mein noodles), cooked following the instructions on the package
2 tablespoons sugar

★ Cut the beef across the grain into thin slices, then stack a few slices one on top of another and cut into slivers the size of long matchsticks. Whisk the eggs with the ¼ cup cornstarch and salt to make a batter. Add the meat. Stir well to coat. Cut the carrot and zucchini into matchsticks.

★ Mix the vinegar and soy sauce in a small bowl. In another bowl, stir together the 1 teaspoon cornstarch and broth or water.

★ Fill a large wok one-quarter full of oil and when the oil is just beginning to smoke, add the carrot and zucchini and deep-fry for 1 minute. Remove with a slotted spoon and transfer to a dish lined with paper towels.

★ Reheat the oil and when starting to smoke, add half the beef, using tongs to make sure the strips of beef remain separate. Deep-fry until crispy, 3 to 5 minutes, then drain and add to the carrot and zucchini. Repeat with the remaining beef.

★ Carefully clean out the wok, add 1 tablespoon fresh oil, and when hot, add the scallions, chile, and garlic. Stir-fry for a few seconds, then add the cooked noodles.

★ Make the sauce by mixing the rice vinegar and soy sauce mixture with the cornstarch and broth mixture; add the sugar. Add to the noodles, then toss in the beef and cooked vegetables. Stir-fry briefly, until heated through.

MAKES 4 PORTIONS

PREPARATION TIME: 12 MINUTES

COOKING TIME: 35 MINUTES

NOT SUITABLE FOR FREEZING

Bow tie bolognese

You could make this with or without the cheeses or just sprinkle with a mix of grated Parmesan and Cheddar and cook under a preheated broiler until golden.

8 ounces farfalle (bow tie) pasta
1 tablespoon olive oil
1 medium red onion, finely chopped
1 red bell pepper, seeded and diced
2 garlic cloves, crushed
12 ounces lean ground beef
½ teaspoon balsamic vinegar
two 14-ounce cans diced tomatoes
2 tablespoons tomato paste
1 tablespoon ketchup
1 bay leaf
2 teaspoons light brown sugar
3 tablespoons chopped fresh basil
8 ounces fresh mozzarella cheese, diced
¼ cup grated Parmesan cheese

★ Cook the pasta following the instructions on the package. Drain.

★ Heat the oil in a large saucepan and sauté the onion and bell pepper for 5 minutes. Add the garlic and sauté for 1 minute. Add the ground beef and sauté, stirring occasionally, until browned. Add the balsamic vinegar and cook for 1 minute until evaporated. Add the canned tomatoes, tomato paste, ketchup, bay leaf, and brown sugar. Bring to a boil, then simmer for 25 minutes. Remove the bay leaf.

★ Preheat the broiler. Add the cooked pasta to the pan along with the basil and mix together. Transfer to a heatproof dish and sprinkle with the mozzarella and Parmesan. Broil for 3 to 4 minutes, until the cheese has melted and is bubbling.

- 🥣 MAKES 4 PORTIONS
- 🕐 PREPARATION TIME: 15 MINUTES
- ⊙ COOKING TIME: 22 MINUTES
- ❄ SUITABLE FOR FREEZING (WITHOUT THE PASTA)

Spicy sausage meatball pasta

You can use any sausages you like, but this recipe works well with spicy ones. There is a huge variety of different flavors in your supermarket. I use ones that have paprika in them, as this adds a smoky flavor to the sauce.

4 fat spicy sausages (Spanish or Italian sausages are best)
2 tablespoons olive oil
1 large onion, finely chopped
2 garlic cloves, crushed
1¼ cups tomato sauce
⅔ cup vegetable or chicken broth
1 teaspoon tomato paste
½ teaspoon sugar
1½ teaspoons fresh thyme or ½ teaspoon dried thyme
8 ounces fusilli pasta
grated Parmesan or Cheddar cheese, to serve

★ Squeeze the sausage meat from the skins into a bowl and shape the meat into 16 to 20 small balls. Heat 1 tablespoon of the oil in a small skillet. Cook the meatballs until lightly golden but still raw in the middle.

★ Heat the remaining 1 tablespoon oil in a large saucepan. Add the onion and garlic and sauté for 4 minutes. Add the tomato sauce, broth, tomato paste, sugar, and thyme and bring to a boil. Add the meatballs, cover, then gently simmer for 10 minutes.

★ Meanwhile, cook the pasta following the instructions on the package. Drain, and add to the sauce.

★ Serve with some grated Parmesan or Cheddar sprinkled on top.

Bow tie pasta with bacon and peas

Simple, cheap, and tasty. A good dish to make when the cupboard is bare.

8 ounces farfalle (bow tie) pasta
1¼ cups frozen peas
4 ounces smoked bacon or pancetta, diced
1 medium onion, finely chopped
½ cup grated Parmesan cheese
2 tablespoons chopped fresh parsley
salt and freshly ground black pepper

★ Cook the pasta following the instructions on the package and add the peas 3 minutes before the end of the cooking time. Drain, reserving ¼ cup of the cooking liquid, and set aside.

★ Cook the bacon in a nonstick skillet for 2 minutes. Add the onion and cook for another 5 minutes. Add the reserved cooking liquid and Parmesan and bring to a boil; then add the pasta and peas along with the parsley and heat through. Season to taste with salt and pepper.

FAVORITE

FISH

◔ MAKES 4 PORTIONS

◔ PREPARATION TIME: 12 MINUTES

◔ COOKING TIME: 15 MINUTES

❋ NOT SUITABLE FOR FREEZING

Creamy cod with penne and shrimp

Cod has been overfished in some parts of the world and is becoming more scarce, so please try to buy fish from sustainable sources. There are some other white fish that would work just as well in this recipe—try pollock or hake. You could also add some peas to the boiling pasta, about 3 minutes before the end of the cooking time.

8 ounces penne pasta
a pat of butter
2 large shallots, finely chopped
1 tablespoon white wine vinegar
⅔ cup fish broth
1 tablespoon cornstarch
scant 1 cup crème fraîche or heavy cream
7 ounces cod fillet, skinned and cut into ¼-inch cubes
6 ounces cooked salad shrimp
2 tablespoons chopped fresh dill
1 large plum tomato, seeded and chopped
½ cup grated Parmesan cheese
salt and freshly ground black pepper

★ Cook the pasta following the instructions on the package. Drain.

★ While the pasta is cooking, melt the butter in a saucepan. Add the shallots and sweat them for 2 to 3 minutes, until soft. Add the vinegar and broth, bring to a boil, and reduce by half. Mix the cornstarch with 2 tablespoons cold water in a small bowl. Add to the broth mixture and stir until thickened. Add the crème fraîche and bring back to a boil.

★ Add the cod, reduce the heat, and simmer gently for 4 minutes. Add the shrimp, dill, and tomato; toss together with the pasta and Parmesan. Season with salt and pepper and serve at once.

- MAKES 4 PORTIONS
- PREPARATION TIME: 20 MINUTES
- COOKING TIME: 42 MINUTES
- SUITABLE FOR FREEZING

Salmon, shrimp, and dill lasagne

Ideally, we should eat oily fish like salmon twice a week. It's good for the heart and good for the brain, so it's good to find new ways to serve it, such as in this tasty lasagne.

4 tablespoons (½ stick) butter
1 leek, trimmed, rinsed, and finely chopped
1½ teaspoons white wine vinegar
5 tablespoons all-purpose flour
2¼ cups whole milk
2 tablespoons lemon juice
4 cups (lightly packed) baby spinach
2 tablespoons chopped fresh dill
¾ cup grated Parmesan cheese
salt and freshly ground black pepper
12 ounces salmon fillet, skinned and cut into ¾-inch cubes
8 ounces shelled large shrimp, cooked
1½ cups small broccoli florets, blanched
6 large sheets fresh lasagne (about 8 ounces), thawed if frozen

★ Preheat the oven to 400°F.

★ Melt the butter in a deep saucepan. Add the leek and gently sauté for 5 to 6 minutes, until soft. Add the vinegar, then stir in the flour and cook over low heat until blended. Add the milk, bring to a boil, then stir until thickened. Add the lemon juice, spinach, dill, and ½ cup of the Parmesan. Stir over low heat until the spinach has wilted. Season with salt and black pepper.

★ Put one-third of the salmon, shrimp, and broccoli into an 8-inch square ovenproof dish. Pour in one-quarter of the sauce. Place 2 sheets of the lasagne on top. Repeat the layers of fish mixture, sauce, and pasta twice, then finish with the last quarter of the sauce.

★ Sprinkle with the remaining ¼ cup Parmesan, then place in the oven for 30 minutes. Let stand for 5 minutes before serving.

Creamy cod with small pasta shells

The wine reduction adds flavor to this dish—but don't worry, all the alcohol evaporates away. If you are using a bouillon cube, make sure you dilute it with the right amount of water; otherwise, this could taste very salty.

1 small onion, finely diced
½ cup white wine
¾ cup fish broth
½ cup heavy cream
½ teaspoon superfine sugar
½ teaspoon lemon juice
2 teaspoons cornstarch
1 teaspoon rice wine vinegar
12 ounces cod fillet, skinned and cut
    into large pieces
2 tablespoons chopped fresh chives
⅔ cup small pasta shells
2 carrots, finely diced
scant 1 cup frozen peas

★ Put the onion and white wine into a saucepan. Bring to a boil and reduce by two-thirds. Add the broth and reduce again by two-thirds. Add the heavy cream, sugar, and lemon juice. Mix the cornstarch with 1 tablespoon cold water, then add it to the hot sauce and stir until thickened.

★ Add the vinegar to the pan, then the cod, and gently simmer for 4 to 5 minutes, until just cooked. Add the chives and gently mix together.

★ Cook the pasta following the instructions on the package. Add the carrots and peas 4 minutes before the end of the cooking time. Drain, spoon a little pasta onto each plate, and spoon the cod and the sauce over the pasta.

Crab linguine

You can buy fresh crabmeat in the supermarket, and by mixing it with sautéed onion, garlic, and chile, you can whip up a great pasta dish in minutes.

6 ounces linguine
2 tablespoons canola oil
¼ cup finely chopped white onion
¼ cup finely chopped red onion
1 garlic clove, crushed
1 teaspoon finely chopped red chile
    (remove seeds for less heat)
6 ounces (about ¾ cup, packed)
    fresh white crabmeat
2 tablespoons fresh chives
salt (preferably sea salt) and freshly
    ground black pepper
1 tablespoon olive oil

★ Cook the linguine following the instructions on the package. Drain.

★ Heat the canola oil in a large saucepan and sauté the onions, garlic, and chile for 3 minutes. Add the crabmeat and cook for 2 minutes.

★ Remove from the heat and stir in the chives. Season with a little salt and a little freshly ground black pepper. Toss with the drained pasta and serve drizzled with the olive oil.

Teriyaki salmon with soba noodles and scallions

Soba noodles are thin Japanese noodles made of buckwheat flour, and in Japan, it is traditionally considered polite to slurp your noodles noisily. This would be fun to serve with child-friendly chopsticks. Mirin is a sweet Japanese rice wine that I use a lot in both salads and marinades; the alcohol will evaporate during cooking.

8 ounces salmon fillet, skinned
3 tablespoons teriyaki sauce
1 teaspoon mirin
1 teaspoon sake
6 ounces soba noodles
½ bunch scallions, thinly sliced
salt and freshly ground black
   pepper

★ Cut the salmon into large cubes. Mix together the teriyaki sauce, mirin, and sake and pour over the salmon. Allow the salmon to marinate in the refrigerator for 20 minutes.

★ Meanwhile, soak 4 bamboo skewers in water so they won't burn during the cooking. Cook the soba noodles in a saucepan of boiling salted water following the instructions on the package. Drain.

★ Preheat the oven to 425°F. Thread the salmon cubes onto the bamboo skewers, reserving the marinade. Bake the salmon skewers in the oven for 8 minutes.

★ Put the reserved marinade in a small saucepan. Bring to a boil, boil for 10 seconds, then remove from the heat and set aside. Do not use the reserved marinade without boiling it first.

★ Fold the scallions into the noodles along with the boiled marinade and season to taste with salt and pepper. Place the salmon skewers on top of the noodles and serve.

VARIATION: Sauté the scallions with a handful of bean sprouts and sugar snap peas or sliced snow peas, stir in 1 tablespoon extra of teriyaki sauce, and toss with the cooked noodles.

- MAKES 6 PORTIONS
- PREPARATION TIME: 12 MINUTES
- COOKING TIME: 10 MINUTES
- NOT SUITABLE FOR FREEZING

Linguine with clams

Also known as *linguine alle vongole,* this dish is prepared by the Italians in two ways: with tomatoes or without. You should cook clams within 24 hours of buying them. Discard clams that are open or have cracked shells. To clean, just before cooking, soak the clams in cold water for 20 minutes, then pull each clam from the water and give the shells a good brushing to remove any additional sand or stubborn debris. Never eat a clam that won't open after cooking.

8 ounces linguine
3 tablespoons olive oil
1 small onion, finely chopped
2 garlic cloves, crushed
a pinch of red pepper flakes
²⁄₃ cup white wine
3 tablespoons chopped fresh
   parsley
1¼ pounds clams
1 tablespoon lemon juice,
   or to taste
salt and freshly ground
   black pepper

★ Cook the linguine in boiling salted water following the instructions on the package. Drain.
★ Heat 2 tablespoons of the oil in a large saucepan. Add the onion and garlic and sauté for 1 minute. Add the red pepper flakes, white wine, parsley, and clams. Cover, bring to a boil, and boil for 4 minutes, or until the shells have opened. Remove the lid and reduce the liquid by half over high heat.
★ Add the pasta to the clam mixture and toss together with the lemon juice, salt, pepper, and the remaining 1 tablespoon oil.

🥣 MAKES 4 PORTIONS

🕐 PREPARATION TIME: 20 MINUTES

◔ COOKING TIME: 15 MINUTES

❄ NOT SUITABLE FOR FREEZING

Spaghetti and mussels in a package

Shop around when buying mussels and select ones with tightly closed shells, avoiding any that are broken. It is best to eat mussels on the same day that you buy them. To clean them, place the mussels in a sink full of cold water and discard any that are open or have cracked shells. Pull away the beards (see page 117) and give the shells a good scrub. Rinse a few times to make sure they are free of sand. Mussels need very little cooking—as soon as the shells are wide open, they are cooked. Cooking them in a package seals in all the delicious flavors.

8 ounces spaghetti
½ red chile, seeded and finely diced
3 garlic cloves, crushed
3 tablespoons chopped fresh
    parsley
2 tablespoons chopped fresh basil
3 tablespoons olive oil
⅓ cup white wine
juice of ½ lemon
½ cup fish broth
1 teaspoon sugar
salt and freshly ground black
    pepper
1 pound mussels, cleaned
grated Parmesan cheese, to
    serve (optional)

★ Preheat the oven to 400°F.

★ Cook the spaghetti in boiling salted water for 1 minute less than the time stated on the package. Drain, refresh with cold water, and set aside in the colander.

★ Mix the chile, garlic, parsley, basil, oil, wine, lemon juice, fish broth, and sugar in a large bowl. Add the spaghetti, season with salt and pepper, and toss together.

★ Divide the pasta among 4 pieces of aluminum foil that each measure 12 inches square. Divide the mussels among the squares and spoon over any sauce remaining in the bowl. Season to taste. Fold in the edges and seal so that each package looks like a half moon.

★ Make a small hole in the top of each package, place the packages on a baking sheet, and bake for 12 to 15 minutes, until hot and the mussels have opened. Open the packages and serve with a little Parmesan cheese, if desired.

- MAKES 4 PORTIONS
- PREPARATION TIME: 18 MINUTES
- COOKING TIME: 25 MINUTES
- NOT SUITABLE FOR FREEZING

Marina's spaghetti with seafood

Seafood with spaghetti is one of my favorite meals. If you have some dry white vermouth, this adds a great flavor to the dish.

1¼ pounds mussels
8 ounces clams
2 tablespoons olive oil
1 medium red onion, sliced
1 garlic clove, crushed
¼ cup dry white vermouth or
    white wine (optional)
one 14-ounce can diced tomatoes
½ cup fish broth
Tabasco sauce
1 teaspoon sugar
salt and freshly ground
    black pepper
8 ounces spaghetti
8 ounces large shrimp, peeled,
    deveined, and thawed if frozen
1 tablespoon chopped fresh basil
1 tablespoon lemon juice

★ Discard any mussels or clams that do not stay closed when gently pressed. Place the mussels and clams in a bowl of salted water for 10 minutes to extract any sand caught in the shells. If the mussel or clam shells still feel gritty after the initial soaking, scrub them under cold running water using a stiff brush. If the mussel or clam shells do not feel gritty after the initial soaking, they don't need to be scrubbed.

★ Use a clean dish towel to wipe the shells clean. Remove the beards from the mussels—these are the little fibrous tufts—by cutting them away with a knife or scissors (some cultivated mussels don't have beards). Place the clams and mussels in a colander and give them a final rinse before using them. If you are not using them immediately, store them in the refrigerator.

★ Heat the olive oil in a large saucepan and sauté the onion and garlic for 7 to 8 minutes, until soft. Add the vermouth or wine, if using, bring to a boil, and reduce by half. Add the diced tomatoes, broth, Tabasco, and sugar, season with salt and black pepper, and cook for 10 minutes.

★ Meanwhile, cook the spaghetti following the instructions on the package. Drain.

★ Add the mussels, clams, shrimp, and basil to the tomato sauce, stir well, cover, and cook for 3 to 4 minutes, until the mussels and clams have opened. Then stir in the cooked spaghetti and the lemon juice just before serving.

MAKES 4 PORTIONS

PREPARATION TIME: 6 MINUTES

COOKING TIME: 10 MINUTES

NOT SUITABLE FOR FREEZING

Branzino with ginger and scallions on a bed of noodles

Branzino is a delicate fish, and the combination of mirin—a sweet rice wine—soy sauce, rice wine vinegar, garlic, and ginger gives it a delicious Japanese flavor. Serve on a bed of noodles with bean sprouts and sugar snap peas for a special occasion. For a spicier version, you can add some chopped red chile when sautéing the garlic and ginger.

2½ tablespoons olive oil
4 branzino fillets, skin on (about 12 ounces)
salt and freshly ground black pepper
one ¾-inch piece of fresh ginger, peeled and thinly sliced
2 garlic cloves
4 ounces sliced sugar snap peas
1¼ cups bean sprouts
a bunch of scallions, thinly sliced
4 ounces medium Chinese egg noodles (chow mein noodles)
¼ cup mirin
¼ cup soy sauce
1 teaspoon rice wine vinegar

★ Heat 1½ tablespoons of the oil in a large skillet. Season the fish with salt and pepper, and score the skin. Sauté the fillets skin side down, over high heat, for 3 to 4 minutes, until crispy. Turn over and cook for 1 minute. Remove to a plate and keep warm.

★ Heat the remaining 1 tablespoon oil. Add the ginger and garlic and sauté for 2 minutes. Add the sugar snap peas, bean sprouts, and half of the scallions and stir-fry for 3 minutes.

★ Cook the noodles following the instructions on the package. Drain, then add to the skillet and season with salt and pepper. Mix together the mirin, soy sauce, and vinegar. Pour half of this sauce over the noodles and heat the rest in a small saucepan. Spoon some noodles onto each plate and place 1 fish fillet on top. Pour the warm sauce over the fish and sprinkle with the remaining scallions. Serve immediately.

Crunchy squid with rigatoni

Kids tend to love deep-fried squid, and if you have never cooked squid before, you'll find that it is really easy and quick. Make sure the squid is fresh, so try to cook it on the day you buy it, and don't overcook, or it can go rubbery. As a variation, instead of using turmeric, try making this with smoked Spanish paprika.

4 ounces rigatoni pasta
4 ounces squid, cleaned, scored, and tentacles removed and cut into rings
¾ cup all-purpose flour
salt and freshly ground black pepper
1 teaspoon ground turmeric
3 tablespoons canola oil
4 ounces sugar snap peas, cut into thin strips

★ Cook the rigatoni following the instructions on the package. Drain.

★ Cut the squid into bite-size pieces. Pour the flour onto a plate, season with salt and pepper, and mix in the turmeric. Coat the squid in the seasoned flour. Heat the oil in a wok. You will know it is hot enough when you drop a cube of bread into the hot oil and it becomes golden and crispy, 50 to 60 seconds. Shake off any excess flour from the squid and sauté the squid for 2 to 3 minutes, until crispy. Don't overcrowd the pan—you can cook this in batches; reheat the oil between each batch, adding extra oil if needed.

★ Meanwhile, blanch the sugar snap peas in boiling salted water, then add to the squid and stir-fry for a few seconds. Mix the pasta with the crunchy squid and sugar snap peas.

◔ MAKES 4 PORTIONS

◷ PREPARATION TIME: 8 MINUTES

☉ COOKING TIME: 8 MINUTES

❄ PESTO SAUCE SUITABLE FOR FREEZING

Spaghetti with pesto

Adding parsley to the mixture helps to give a good green color. You could add a few chopped sun-dried tomatoes to the spaghetti, too, or sprinkle with some pine nuts.

8 ounces spaghetti

GREEN PESTO SAUCE
⅓ cup pine nuts
½ cup grated Parmesan cheese, plus extra for serving
1 or 2 garlic cloves
a small bunch of parsley leaves
a small bunch of basil leaves and stalks
a pinch of sugar
scant ½ cup olive oil
salt and freshly ground black pepper

★ Cook the spaghetti following the instructions on the package.
★ Meanwhile, toast the pine nuts in a dry skillet until lightly golden. Remove from the pan and let cool.
★ Combine the ½ cup Parmesan, garlic, parsley, basil, sugar, and cooled pine nuts in a food processor and whiz until finely chopped. Slowly add the olive oil while the motor is running. Add 1 tablespoon water and season with salt and pepper. Spoon the pesto into a small bowl.
★ Drain the cooked pasta and put it back into the pot. Add 4 to 5 tablespoons of the pesto and toss together.
★ Sprinkle with extra Parmesan before serving.
(You can freeze any leftover pesto sauce for up to 2 months.)

Spinach, ricotta, and tomato lasagne

TOMATO SAUCE
2 tablespoons olive oil
1 large onion, chopped
1 garlic clove, crushed
1 tablespoon balsamic vinegar
two 14-ounce cans diced tomatoes
2 tablespoons chopped oil-packed
    sun-dried tomatoes
2 tablespoons tomato paste

SPINACH AND RICOTTA FILLING
1 tablespoon olive oil
½ small onion, chopped
1¼ pounds fresh spinach, washed
    and tough stalks removed
1 cup ricotta cheese
2 tablespoons grated Parmesan
    cheese
salt and freshly ground black pepper

CHEESE SAUCE
2 tablespoons butter
3 tablespoons all-purpose flour
1¾ cups milk
¾ cup grated Gruyère cheese
salt and freshly ground black pepper

9 sheets fresh lasagne (about
    12 ounces), thawed if frozen
¼ cup grated Parmesan cheese

★ Preheat the oven to 350°F.

★ To make the tomato sauce, heat the oil in a saucepan and sauté the onion and garlic for 4 minutes. Add the balsamic vinegar and cook for about 30 seconds. Drain half the juice from the diced tomatoes and add the tomatoes, sun-dried tomatoes, and tomato paste to the onion. Bring to a boil and simmer for 10 minutes.

★ Meanwhile, make the filling: Heat the oil in a saucepan and sauté the onion for 4 minutes, or until softened. Stir in the spinach and cook until wilted, transfer to a strainer, then squeeze out the excess water. Transfer the spinach to a bowl, mix with the ricotta cheese and the 2 tablespoons Parmesan, and chop for a few seconds in a food processor. Season with a little salt and pepper. Set aside.

★ For the cheese sauce, melt the butter, stir in the flour, and cook for about 1 minute. Gradually stir in the milk and cook for about 2 minutes, or until thickened. Stir in the grated Gruyère until melted and season to taste with salt and pepper.

★ You may need to cook the lasagne in lightly salted boiling water first; follow the instructions on the package.

★ To assemble the lasagne, spoon one-third of the tomato sauce into the bottom of a fairly deep ovenproof dish (with 3-inch sides) and cover with a layer of the spinach and ricotta mixture. Cover with 3 sheets of lasagne followed by a layer of tomato sauce. Repeat with each layer twice, finishing off with a layer of the cheese sauce.

★ Sprinkle with the ¼ cup Parmesan cheese and bake for 30 minutes.

⌣ MAKES 4 PORTIONS

⏱ PREPARATION TIME: 15 MINUTES

☉ COOKING TIME: 15 MINUTES

❄ NOT SUITABLE FOR FREEZING

⌣ MAKES 6 PORTIONS

⏱ PREPARATION TIME: 8 MINUTES

☉ COOKING TIME: 45 MINUTES

❄ NOT SUITABLE FOR FREEZING

Vegetable fusilli

8 ounces fusilli pasta
½ cup frozen peas
1 tablespoon olive oil
1 large onion, finely chopped
1 garlic clove, crushed
1 small yellow bell pepper, cut into strips
1 cup small broccoli florets
1 medium zucchini, cut into matchsticks
½ cup crème fraîche or heavy cream
½ cup vegetable broth
¾ cup grated Parmesan cheese, plus extra to serve (optional)
salt and freshly ground black pepper
6 to 8 ripe medium tomatoes, peeled, seeded, and chopped

★ Cook the pasta following the instructions on the package and add the peas 4 minutes before the end of the cooking time. Drain the pasta and peas. Set aside.

★ Heat the olive oil in a large saucepan and sauté the onion and garlic for 1 minute. Add the bell pepper, broccoli, and zucchini and sauté for about 8 minutes, or just until tender. Stir in the crème fraîche and the vegetable broth. Bring to a boil and reduce by one-third. Add the Parmesan and season with salt and pepper. Then add the tomatoes and simmer for 1 minute.

★ Add the drained pasta and peas, then toss together. Serve with extra Parmesan to sprinkle on top if desired.

Grandma's noodle pudding

8 ounces vermicelli or fine egg noodles
1 large egg, beaten
2 tablespoons butter, melted, plus extra for topping
scant ½ cup milk
2 tablespoons superfine sugar
1 teaspoon vanilla extract
½ teaspoon pumpkin pie spice
¾ cup each dark and golden raisins
3 tablespoons sliced almonds (optional)

★ Preheat the oven to 350°F.

★ Cook the vermicelli or fine egg noodles following the instructions on the package. Drain. Mix with all of the remaining ingredients except the extra butter.

★ Pour the mixture into a greased shallow 9-inch square baking dish. Dot with the extra butter and bake for 40 minutes.

🥣 MAKES 2 PORTIONS

🕐 PREPARATION TIME: 6 MINUTES

☉ COOKING TIME: 10 MINUTES

❊ NOT SUITABLE FOR FREEZING

🥣 MAKES 6 PORTIONS

🕐 PREPARATION TIME: 10 MINUTES

☉ COOKING TIME: 40 MINUTES

❊ SUITABLE FOR FREEZING

Field, flat, and wild mushroom tagliatelle

6 ounces tagliatelle pasta
1 tablespoon olive oil
1 medium onion, diced
1 garlic clove, chopped
1 cup sliced cremini mushrooms
1¼ cups sliced portobello mushrooms
¾ cup sliced wild or shiitake mushrooms
½ cup crème fraîche or heavy cream
2 teaspoons chopped chives
salt and freshly ground black pepper

★ Cook the tagliatelle following the instructions on the package. Drain.

★ Heat the oil in a large skillet and sauté the onion, garlic, and mushrooms for 5 minutes. Add the crème fraîche and simmer for 1 minute. Fold in the chopped chives and season to taste with salt and pepper.

★ Serve the drained tagliatelle with the sauce poured over.

Lentil soup with pasta

2 tablespoons olive oil
1 large leek, trimmed, rinsed, and
    roughly chopped
1 large celery stalk, roughly chopped
1 large carrot, finely diced
¾ cup split red lentils
2 garlic cloves, crushed
one 14-ounce can diced tomatoes
6 cups chicken broth
2 tablespoons tomato paste
⅓ cup small pasta shells
2 tablespoons chopped fresh thyme
1 tablespoon chopped fresh parsley
salt and freshly ground black pepper

★ Heat the oil in a deep saucepan. Add the leek, celery, and carrot and sauté for 5 minutes. Add the lentils, garlic, tomatoes, chicken broth, and tomato paste. Bring to a boil and simmer for 25 minutes, or until the lentils are just cooked.

★ Add the pasta and continue to simmer for 8 to 9 minutes, until the pasta is cooked. Add the thyme and parsley and season to taste with salt and pepper.

MAKES 4 PORTIONS

PREPARATION TIME: 1 HOUR

COOKING TIME: 5 MINUTES

SUITABLE FOR FREEZING

Spinach and ricotta ravioli

PASTA
scant 2½ cups double-zero
   (oo) flour, plus extra for dusting
3 large eggs
1 teaspoon salt
1 tablespoon olive oil

FILLING
8 ounces baby spinach
scant ½ cup ricotta cheese
½ cup grated Parmesan cheese
1 egg yolk, lightly beaten
a pinch of nutmeg

SAUCE
3 tablespoons olive oil
1 large garlic clove, crushed
5 large ripe tomatoes, peeled,
   seeded, and roughly chopped

★ Make the pasta: Measure the 2½ cups flour, the eggs, salt, and oil into a bowl. Mix with a wooden spoon, then knead with your hands to form a dough. Knead on a floured work surface for 10 minutes, or until shiny and smooth. Cover with plastic wrap and let rest for 10 minutes at room temperature.

★ Divide the dough into 4 balls. Roll out 1 ball into a small rectangle, then feed it through a pasta machine, starting with the widest setting. Go through each setting 2 or 3 times, working up from thickest to thinnest. Sprinkle flour over the sheet occasionally so it doesn't stick.

★ Cut the long sheet of pasta in half; the 2 sheets should be about 12 by 4 inches. Repeat with the remaining 3 balls until you have 8 sheets. Dust with flour, then place on a baking sheet dusted with flour. Cover with plastic wrap and let rest for 10 minutes.

★ Heat 1 tablespoon water in a skillet, add the spinach, and cook until wilted. Put into a bowl and let cool; stir in the remaining filling ingredients. Put 1 sheet of pasta on the work surface and spoon 6 teaspoons of filling along it. Brush a little water around each spoonful, put another sheet on top, and press down around the filling to seal the edges. Cut around the mounds to make 6 squares, crimping the edges with a fork. Dust with flour and let dry for 30 minutes, turning halfway. Make 24 squares.

★ Heat the oil in a saucepan. Add the garlic and tomatoes and warm through. Cook the ravioli in boiling salted water for 3 to 4 minutes, until the pasta is just cooked. Drain, then serve with the sauce.

- MAKES 4 PORTIONS
- PREPARATION TIME: 1 HOUR
- COOKING TIME: 5 MINUTES
- SUITABLE FOR FREEZING

Butternut squash ravioli

FILLING
¾ cup peeled and roughly chopped
   butternut squash
3 tablespoons ricotta cheese
2 tablespoons grated Parmesan
   cheese
½ teaspoon chopped fresh sage
half a lightly beaten egg yolk
salt and freshly ground black
   pepper

1 recipe ravioli pasta (see page 128)

TO SERVE
3 tablespoons fresh pesto
   (see page 122) or good-quality
   store-bought

★ To make the filling, steam the butternut squash in a steamer for 10 to 12 minutes, until soft. Let cool. Mash the squash in a bowl using a fork. Add the ricotta, Parmesan, sage, and egg yolk, and season with salt and pepper.

★ Make the ravioli as in the recipe on page 128, making 24 squares.

★ Cook the ravioli in boiling salted water for 3 to 4 minutes, until the pasta is just cooked. Drain, then gently toss with the pesto.

🥣 MAKES 4 PORTIONS

🕐 PREPARATION TIME: 1 HOUR

◉ COOKING TIME: 20 MINUTES

❄ SUITABLE FOR FREEZING

Three-cheese ravioli

FILLING
¼ cup ricotta cheese
½ cup finely grated Parmesan cheese
½ cup finely grated Gruyère cheese
1 egg yolk, lightly beaten
salt and freshly ground black pepper

1 recipe ravioli pasta (see page 128)

TOMATO SAUCE
1 tablespoon olive oil
1 medium onion, chopped
1 garlic clove, crushed
one 14-ounce can diced tomatoes
1 teaspoon tomato paste
a pinch of sugar

★ Mix the ricotta, Parmesan, Gruyère, and egg yolk together in a bowl and season well with salt and pepper.

★ Make the ravioli as in the recipe on page 128, making 24 squares.

★ To make the sauce, heat the oil in a saucepan, add the onion and garlic, and sauté for 5 minutes. Add the tomatoes, ½ cup water, tomato paste, and sugar. Cover and simmer for 15 to 20 minutes, until slightly thickened, then whiz with a handheld blender until smooth.

★ Cook the ravioli in boiling salted water for 3 to 4 minutes, until the pasta is just cooked. Drain, then toss with the sauce.

- 🥣 MAKES 4 PORTIONS
- 🕐 PREPARATION TIME: 30 MINUTES
- ☉ COOKING TIME: 1 HOUR 20 MINUTES
- ❄ SUITABLE FOR FREEZING

Pumpkin gnocchi with lemon-sage butter sauce

14 ounces Yukon Gold potatoes
8 ounces sweet potatoes
½ small pumpkin or medium butternut squash (about 10 ounces), seeded and cut into wedges
a pat of butter
scant 1 cup all-purpose flour, plus extra for dusting
1 egg yolk, lightly beaten
salt and freshly ground black pepper
4 cups vegetable broth

LEMON-SAGE BUTTER SAUCE
2 tablespoons olive oil
1 small onion, finely chopped
2 tablespoons fresh sage leaves, thinly sliced
½ cup (1 stick) unsalted butter
finely grated zest of 1 lemon
salt and freshly ground black pepper

★ Preheat the oven to 350°F.

★ Prick the potatoes all over using a fork. Place on a large baking sheet with the pumpkin or butternut squash wedges, skin side down. Melt the butter and use it to brush the flesh of the pumpkin or butternut squash. Bake the vegetables for 1 hour, or until they are tender. Remove from the oven and let cool.

★ Cut the potatoes in half and scoop the flesh into a bowl, along with that of the pumpkin or butternut squash. Either put the vegetables through a food mill or mash thoroughly and put into a large bowl. Sift in the flour, add the egg yolk, and mix with a wooden spoon. Season with salt and pepper.

★ Fit a piping bag with a ¾-inch tip and fill with some of the mixture. Pipe lengths of gnocchi onto a floured baking sheet, then cut into ¾-inch pieces before poaching in boiling vegetable broth, or squeeze the mixture out of the piping bag and cut into 1-inch lengths so that the pieces drop straight into the boiling broth. Cook for about 1 minute, until the gnocchi float to the surface. Remove them carefully with a slotted spoon and arrange them on a baking sheet. You will need to cook the gnocchi in about 4 batches.

★ To make the lemon-sage butter sauce, heat the oil and sauté the onion for 3 to 4 minutes, until softened but not colored. Add the sage and sauté for 30 seconds. Stir in the butter until melted, then remove from the heat and stir in the lemon zest. Season to taste with salt and pepper. Serve the gnocchi with the lemon-sage butter drizzled on top.

MAKES 4 PORTIONS

PREPARATION TIME: 15 MINUTES

COOKING TIME: 30 MINUTES

NOT SUITABLE FOR FREEZING

Spaghetti with tomato, mozzarella, and spinach

1 tablespoon olive oil
6 cups (lightly packed) baby spinach
salt and freshly ground black pepper
½ medium red onion, finely chopped
1 red chile, seeded and finely diced
2 garlic cloves, crushed
one 14-ounce can whole plum
   tomatoes
1 tablespoon light brown sugar
1 tablespoon ketchup
1 tablespoon tomato paste
8 ounces spaghetti
2 large fresh plum tomatoes,
   seeded and roughly chopped
8 ounces fresh mozzarella, diced
2 tablespoons roughly chopped basil

★ Heat 1 teaspoon of the oil in a wok or deep skillet. Sauté the spinach for 2 to 3 minutes, until wilted. Season with salt and pepper and set aside.

★ Heat the remaining 2 teaspoons oil in the wok and sauté the onion for 6 to 8 minutes. Add the chile and garlic and sauté for 1 minute. Add the canned tomatoes, sugar, ketchup, and tomato paste, then reduce the sauce over medium heat for 10 to 12 minutes, until thickened.

★ Cook the spaghetti following the instructions on the package. Drain.

★ Add the fresh tomatoes to the tomato sauce along with the spinach and cook for 3 to 4 minutes, until the fresh tomatoes soften slightly.

★ Add the drained pasta. Toss together and season well with salt and pepper. Add the mozzarella and basil and serve.

Mushroom and ricotta cheese cannelloni with pesto

FILLING

1 tablespoon olive oil
1 medium onion, finely chopped
1 garlic clove, crushed
3½ cups chopped cremini mushrooms
1 cup ricotta cheese
1 egg yolk, lightly beaten
heaping ¾ cup grated Parmesan
  cheese
salt and freshly ground black pepper

12 no-preboil cannelloni tubes

TOMATO SAUCE

one 14-ounce can diced tomatoes
2 tablespoons tomato paste
2 tablespoons chopped fresh thyme
  leaves

PESTO SAUCE

4 tablespoons (½ stick) butter
heaping ⅓ cup all-purpose flour
2½ cups milk
salt and freshly ground black pepper
3 tablespoons fresh pesto (see
  page 122) or good-quality store-
  bought
1 cup grated Parmesan cheese

★ Preheat the oven to 350°F.

★ First, make the filling: Heat the oil in a saucepan and sauté the onion for 5 to 6 minutes, until soft. Add the garlic and mushrooms and continue to sauté for another 5 minutes, or until the mushrooms are cooked and the pan is dry. Transfer to a bowl and let cool. When cool, add the ricotta, egg yolk, and Parmesan and season with salt and pepper. Using your hands or a spoon, stuff the cannelloni tubes with the mixture.

★ Make the tomato sauce by simply mixing together all the sauce ingredients in a bowl.

★ Finally, make the pesto sauce: Melt the butter in a saucepan. Add the flour and stir over medium heat for 1 minute. Add the milk slowly, stirring until blended. Bring to a boil, then reduce the heat to a simmer and cook for 2 minutes. Season with salt and pepper, then add the pesto and ½ cup of the Parmesan.

★ Spoon the tomato sauce onto the bottom of an ovenproof dish. Place the filled cannelloni tubes on top in a single layer. Pour the pesto sauce over the cannelloni so they are completely covered. Sprinkle the remaining ½ cup Parmesan on top. Bake for 40 minutes, or until the top is golden brown and the pasta is soft.

- MAKES 6 PORTIONS
- PREPARATION TIME: 1 HOUR
- COOKING TIME: 12 MINUTES
- SUITABLE FOR FREEZING

Fresh spinach tagliatelle

PASTA
4 cups (lightly packed) baby
    spinach
scant 2½ cups double-zero
    (oo) flour, plus extra for dusting
2 eggs, lightly beaten
1 egg yolk, lightly beaten
1 tablespoon olive oil
1 teaspoon salt

4 to 6 tablespoons butter
salt and freshly ground black
    pepper
½ cup finely grated Parmesan
    cheese

★ Put the spinach into a skillet with 1 tablespoon water. Cook over high heat until wilted. Drain, squeeze out most of the liquid, finely chop, and let cool. Put the remaining pasta ingredients into a bowl with the spinach. Mix with a wooden spoon, then knead with your hands to form a dough. Knead on a floured work surface for 10 minutes, or until shiny and smooth. (You can make the dough in a freestanding mixer with a dough hook. Measure all the dough ingredients into the bowl and mix until they have formed a ball. Knead at low speed for 5 to 6 minutes, until the dough is smooth.) Cover with plastic wrap and let rest for 30 minutes at room temperature.

★ Divide the dough into 4 balls. Roll out 1 ball into a small rectangle using a rolling pin. Feed through a pasta machine, starting with the widest setting. Go through each setting 2 or 3 times, working up from thickest to thinnest. Sprinkle the sheet with flour occasionally. Repeat with the remaining pasta until you have 4 long sheets.

★ Divide each sheet into 2, so you have 8 sheets in total. Hang the sheets on a pasta stand with wooden posts to rest for 10 minutes. Carefully feed the sheets through the tagliatelle cutter on the pasta machine. Dust with flour, then place on a baking sheet dusted with a little flour. Cover with plastic wrap until needed.

★ Bring a pot of salted water to a boil. Add the pasta and boil for 1½ to 2 minutes, until the pasta is just cooked. Drain. Add the butter to the hot pot and gently melt. Add the pasta, salt, pepper, and half of the Parmesan. Toss together and serve with the remaining cheese scattered on top.

MAKES 4 TO 5 PORTIONS

PREPARATION TIME: 25 MINUTES

COOKING TIME: 1 HOUR

SUITABLE FOR FREEZING

Vegetarian pasta bake with a crunchy topping

1 tablespoon olive oil
1 medium eggplant, cut into
    ¾-inch cubes
1 red bell pepper, seeded and cut
    into ½-inch cubes
1 large zucchini, cut into ½-inch
    cubes
1 medium red onion, cut into
    wedges
1¼ cups sliced cremini mushrooms
2 garlic cloves, crushed
½ red chile, seeded and finely diced
one 14-ounce can diced tomatoes
1¼ cups vegetable broth
1 tablespoon tomato paste
½ cup grated sharp Cheddar
    cheese
8 ounces fresh mozzarella, diced
6 sheets fresh lasagne (about
    8 ounces), thawed if frozen
1 cup fresh bread crumbs
⅓ cup sunflower seeds

★ Preheat the oven to 400°F.

★ Heat the oil in a deep skillet, add the eggplant, and sauté over high heat for 4 to 5 minutes, until lightly golden. Add the bell pepper, zucchini, onion, mushrooms, garlic, and chile and sauté for another 5 minutes. Add the tomatoes, broth, and tomato paste. Bring to a boil, cover, and simmer for 20 to 25 minutes, until the vegetables are soft and the liquid has thickened.

★ Spoon one-quarter of the sauce into an ovenproof dish. Sprinkle with a little Cheddar and mozzarella. Place 2 sheets of the lasagne on top. Repeat so you have 3 layers of pasta and 4 layers of tomato-and-vegetable sauce. Sprinkle the last layer of sauce with the bread crumbs, then top with the sunflower seeds.

★ Bake for 25 to 30 minutes, until golden on top and the pasta is cooked in the middle.

MAKES 3 PORTIONS

PREP TIME: 8 MINUTES, PLUS 1 HOUR MARINATING

COOKING TIME: 8 MINUTES

NOT SUITABLE FOR FREEZING

MAKES 2 PORTIONS

PREPARATION TIME: 6 MINUTES

COOKING TIME: 24 MINUTES

SAUCE SUITABLE FOR FREEZING

Spaghettini with tomato salsa

TOMATO SALSA
6 large ripe tomatoes, seeded and roughly chopped
¼ to ½ red chile, seeded and finely chopped
½ medium red onion, finely diced
1 small garlic clove, crushed
6 oil-packed sun-dried tomatoes, chopped
a small bunch of fresh basil, roughly chopped
2 tablespoons white wine vinegar

salt and freshly ground black pepper
8 ounces spaghettini
grated Parmesan cheese, to serve

★ Measure all the salsa ingredients into a large bowl, season with salt and pepper, and set aside to marinate for 1 hour at room temperature.
★ Cook the spaghettini following the instructions on the package. Drain, then add to the salsa ingredients. Toss together in the bowl until coated and serve with some freshly grated Parmesan.

Easy tomato sauce

1 ½ tablespoons olive oil
1 medium onion, chopped
1 garlic clove, crushed
one 14-ounce can diced tomatoes
1 tablespoon tomato paste
1 tablespoon ketchup
1 teaspoon sugar
6 ounces spaghetti or fusilli pasta
8 large basil leaves
salt and freshly ground black pepper

★ Heat the oil in a saucepan. Add the onion and garlic and sauté for 4 minutes. Add the tomatoes, tomato paste, ketchup, and sugar. Bring to a boil, cover, and simmer for 20 minutes.
★ Meanwhile, cook the pasta following the instructions on the package. Drain.
★ Tear the basil into pieces and stir into the tomato sauce. Season with salt and pepper and toss the pasta with the tomato sauce.

index

about the author

Annabel Karmel is the bestselling author of thirty-nine books on nutrition and cooking for babies, children, and the whole family. The UK's leading expert on feeding children and the mother of three, Annabel has appeared on the *Today* show, *Live with Regis and Kelly*, and *The View*. She has her own very popular line of meals for children in supermarkets across the UK and has co-branded a range of foods for young children with Disney. She was awarded an MBE in the Queen's Honour List for her outstanding work in the field of child nutrition. For more recipes and advice, visit www.annabelkarmel.com.

Annabel Karmel: Healthy Baby and Toddler Recipes, **with 100 recipes and videos, is available from the App store, www.annabelkarmel.com.**

acknowledgments

Thanks to my children, Nicholas, Lara, and Scarlett, who have eaten their way through this book. Thanks to Lucinda Kaizik and Caroline Brewster for their assistance in the kitchen and on the page; Seiko Hatfield, my wonderful food stylist; Dave King for his stunning photography and Jo Harris for the props. Thanks to the team at Atria: Judith Curr, Greer Hendricks, Sarah Cantin, Sybil Pincus, Cristina Suarez, Rachel Zugschwert, and Chris Lloreda.

www.annabelkarmel.com